D0983828

Writing the Critical Essay

MILITARY DRAFT

An OPPOSING VIEWPOINTS® Guide

Lauri S. Friedman, *Book Editor*

Christine Nasso, *Publisher*
Elizabeth Des Chenes, *Managing Editor*

OPPOSING
VIEWPOINTS®
SERIES

GREENHAVEN PRESS
An imprint of Thomson Gale, a part of The Thomson Corporation

THOMSON
™
GALE

Detroit • New York • San Francisco • New Haven, Conn. • Waterville, Maine • London

LIBRARY OF CONGRESS CATALOGING-IN-PUBLICATION DATA

Military draft / Lauri S. Friedman, book editor.
    p. cm. — (Writing the critical essay)
  Includes bibliographical references and index.
  ISBN-13: 978-0-7377-3858-2 (hardcover.)
  1. Draft—United States. 2. Essay—Authorship. 3. Rhetoric. I. Friedman, Lauri S.
  UB343.M493 2007
  808'.066355—dc22

                                                        2007032512

ISBN-10: 0-7377-3858-8 (hardcover.)
Printed in the United States of America

CONTENTS

E xamining the state of writing and how it is taught in the United States was the official purpose of the National Commission on Writing in America's Schools and Colleges. The commission, made up of teachers, school administrators, business leaders, and college and university presidents, released its first report in 2003. "Despite the best efforts of many educators," commissioners argued, "writing has not received the full attention it deserves." Among the findings of the commission was that most fourth-grade students spent less than three hours a week writing, that three-quarters of high school seniors never receive a writing assignment in their history or social studies classes, and that more than 50 percent of first-year students in college have problems writing error-free papers. The commission called for a "cultural sea change" that would increase the emphasis on writing for both elementary and secondary schools. These conclusions have made some educators realize that writing must be emphasized in the curriculum. As colleges are demanding an ever-higher level of writing proficiency from incoming students, schools must respond by making students more competent writers. In response to these concerns, the SAT, an influential standardized test used for college admissions, required an essay for the first time in 2005.

Books in the Writing the Critical Essay: An Opposing Viewpoints Guide series use the patented Opposing Viewpoints format to help students learn to organize ideas and arguments and to write essays using common critical writing techniques. Each book in the series focuses on a particular type of essay writing—including expository, persuasive, descriptive, and narrative—that students learn while being taught both the five-paragraph essay as well as longer pieces of writing that have an opinionated focus. These guides include everything necessary to help students research, outline, draft, edit, and ultimately write successful essays across the curriculum, including essays for the SAT.

Using Opposing Viewpoints

This series is inspired by and builds upon Greenhaven Press's acclaimed Opposing Viewpoints series. As in the parent series, each book in the Writing the Critical Essay series focuses on a timely and controversial social issue that provides lots of opportunities for creating thought-provoking essays. The first section of each volume begins with a brief introductory essay that provides context for the opposing viewpoints that follow. These articles are chosen for their accessibility and clearly stated views. The thesis of each article is made explicit in the article's title and is accentuated by its pairing with an opposing or alternative view. These essays are both models of persuasive writing techniques and valuable research material that students can mine to write their own informed essays. Guided reading and discussion questions help lead students to key ideas and writing techniques presented in the selections.

The second section of each book begins with a preface discussing the format of the essays and examining characteristics of the featured essay type. Model five-paragraph and longer essays then demonstrate that essay type. The essays are annotated so that key writing elements and techniques are pointed out to the student. Sequential, step-by-step exercises help students construct and refine thesis statements; organize material into outlines; analyze and try out writing techniques; write transitions, introductions, and conclusions; and incorporate quotations and other researched material. Ultimately, students construct their own compositions using the designated essay type.

The third section of each volume provides additional research material and writing prompts to help the student. Additional facts about the topic of the book serve as a convenient source of supporting material for essays. Other features help students go beyond the book for their research. Like other Greenhaven Press books, each book in the Writing the Critical Essay series includes bibliographic listings of relevant periodical articles, books, Web sites, and organizations to contact.

Writing the Critical Essay: An Opposing Viewpoints Guide will help students master essay techniques that can be used in any discipline.

Can the All-Volunteer Force Meet the Military Needs of the Twenty-First Century?

Much of the United States' twentieth century military history was based on conscription, or compulsive military service. The idea behind conscription, or what is popularly referred to as "the draft," is that every American should hold an equal responsibility for defending their country. In other words, because everyone shares in America's wealth, opportunity, and freedoms, every citizen should be required to make sacrifices to defend these rights.

Yet as the wars of the twentieth century came and went it became clear that the draft did not result in an equitable or even efficient military division. Increasing opposition to the morality of the Vietnam War, as well as complaints that the draft was easy for the privileged to either dodge or serve in partial capacity, led thousands of young men eligible for conscription to either burn their draft cards or flee to Canada. After a series of lawsuits in the early 1970s, the draft was eventually abolished in 1973. It was replaced with an all-volunteer military, which continues to be the basis of the U.S. military today.

The benefit of the AVF, it was believed, was that if soldiers served by choice, they would be more motivated, better qualified, and more committed than those who were forced into service. Indeed, since 1973, the All-Volunteer Force (AVF) has resulted in a strong military that does not force citizens to serve. But in recent years, and especially since the declaration of the War on Terror and the 2003 War in Iraq, opinions have varied widely about whether the AVF

President Roosevelt signs the first peace-time draft law on September 16, 1940, which called for men over the age of twenty-one to train and serve in the armed forces.

has helped or hindered America's military readiness and whether it is the best option for meeting the military challenges of the twenty-first century.

According to some, the AVF remains the best option for maintaining a strong, dependable, and skilled military. Today's military offers soldiers the chance to learn in depth about computers, engineering, and heavy industrial equipment—experience that will help them get a job or return to school after they serve. The scope of opportunities for today's recruits has made the military an especially attractive option for young men and women. A senior Defense Department official explained during a briefing on the AVF: "In the draft era, we largely told you what was good for you... 'you're going to like this military occupation... it builds character.' Now we come to [recruits] and say, 'Well, which of these ... training opportunities would entice you to join and stay with us?'"[1] Indeed, President George W. Bush has rejected efforts to reinstate the draft, arguing that "our country's all-volunteer force attracts idealistic and committed young Americans. They stay in service longer because they have chosen the military life. The result is a military with the highest level of training and experience, motivation, and professionalism."[2]

But in the twenty first century, the all-volunteer military is also forced to deal with warfare that, unlike past battles, has no clearly defined beginning and end. The skills that many soldiers have learned are best applied to concrete, defined missions, and thus may not be entirely appropriate for fighting the War on Terror in the varied places and lengths of time required. Conventional combat training may not prepare recruits for just how uniquely intense these current conflicts can be.

These realities, compounded by a very politically charged climate, have decreased Americans' willingness to serve their country. For example, in 2005 the branches of the military repeatedly missed their monthly recruiting goals, and by the end of the year had suffered the worst recruiting results since 1979. Interest in all branches of the military was dangerously low—by April alone the Army had fallen short of its required number of recruits by 42 percent. Compounding

[1] Background Briefing on the All Volunteer Force, January 13, 2003. http://www.defenselink.mil/transcripts/transcript.aspx?transcriptid=1252
[2] George W. Bush, Remarks by the President at Reenlistment of Military Service Members, July 1, 2003. http://www.whitehouse.gov/news/releases/2003/07/20030701-9.html

the lack of interest in serving was a need for more troops. Bogged down in conflicts in Afghanistan and Iraq, and facing a potential future conflict with Iran, the Army estimated it needed to add at least 50,000 soldiers to the million-strong army, but was nowhere close to achieving this number.

Therefore, reinstating the military draft has been suggested as a way to meet required numbers in a time when Americans are less than willing to volunteer for service. As *New York Times* columnist Bob Herbert has written, "The all-volunteer army is fine in peacetime, and in military routs like the first gulf war. But when the troops are locked in a prolonged war that yields high casualties, and they look over their shoulders to see if reinforcements are coming from the general population, they find—as they're finding now—that no one is there."[3]

But lessons from the past show that forcing people to serve when they don't want to can have disastrous results, including apathetic, unmotivated, poorly trained soldiers and political upheaval at home. Furthermore, shoving all types of people with varied skill sets into the same, rotating service regime would likely harm the very qualities of the American military that make it so world renown. As military historian Winston Groom has argued, "If you begin drafting people into the armed forces again, you can probably train them to shoot a rifle, salute, march and drill, load an artillery piece, or swab the deck of a ship, just like in the old days. But the old days are gone. You won't get the dedication and special ability of the professionals we already have. What you will get instead is a gigantic, useless mob of half-trained malcontents whose skills are half-a-century outdated. The world already has too many militaries like that."[4]

Whether the U.S. needs a military draft is an ongoing debate, and one that gains importance with each passing

[3] Bob Herbert, "The Army's Hard Sell," *New York Times*, June 27, 2005.
[4] Winston Groom, "An Army of 50 Million? The Surpassingly Dishonest Draft Debate," *Weekly Standard*, December 11, 2006.

year of the War on Terror and other twenty-first century conflicts. The articles and model essays included in *Writing the
Critical Essay: An Opposing Viewpoints Guide: The Military
Draft* expose readers to the basic arguments made about the
military draft and help them develop tools to craft their own
essays on the subject.

*Police forces were
once required to escort
draftees to induction
centers due to threats
of violence from war
protesters.*

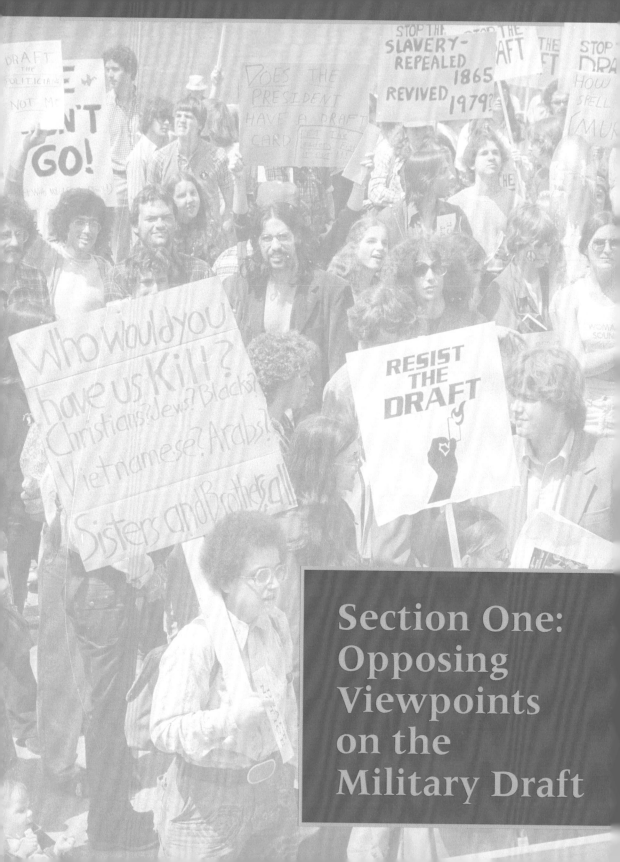

Section One:
Opposing
Viewpoints
on the
Military Draft

The United States Should Reinstate the Draft

Walt Shotwell

In the following viewpoint, author Walt Shotwell argues the United States should bring back the military draft. He lays out his vision of the draft, explaining it should require all high school graduates to serve for at least 2 years either abroad or at home in a variety of different capacities. Draftees would undergo basic training which would include learning valuable skills, new technologies, and new languages. Such a system, argues the author, would enable the United States to have the resources and manpower to adequately fight the war on terror, bring down the national deficit, and inspire camaraderie in all American citizens. For these reasons, Shotwell believes reinstating the military draft is critical to solving several of America's problems.

Walt Shotwell is a former reporter for the Des Moines Register. His articles have also appeared in *Cityview*, Des Moines' alternative newspaper covering central Iowa, from which this viewpoint was taken.

Consider the Following Questions:

1. What types of appointments does the author think should be part of a national service program?
2. According to the author, how many nations have the draft?
3. In what ways does the author believe a draft can save the country money?

Walt Shotwell, "We Need Universal Service Now," *Cityview*, vol. 14, March 9, 2006, p. 11. Reproduced by permission.

While awaiting the next terrorist attack or natural disaster, the United States should initiate a period of mandatory national service. Many leaders say we live in a world where no one is safe, but most Americans are going their merry ways as though no threat exists. The concept that we are all in this together has not materialized as it did in World War II. A period of national service, as distinguished from a military draft, should be initiated now.

The Draft Would Improve America

Besides uniting Americans as never before, national service would be a giant step toward correcting America's dirty little secret that was exposed when Hurricane Katrina uprooted thousands of New Orleans residents living in squalid poverty. Their misery was televised worldwide, much to the dismay of other nations. Besides New Orleans, the television host, Oprah Winfrey, found grim poverty only 70 miles from her Chicago studio. A period of national service would spring thousands of young Americans from poverty by giving them opportunities outside the ghettos.

Compulsory national service is not a new idea. Still, essentially without exception, elected officials are afraid to propose such a politically sensitive issue because it smacks of a military draft. This is not a valid concern; most participants in national service would not be trained to fight.

A Variety of Services for a Variety of Needs

All high school graduates would serve their country for, say, two years. Some would, indeed, want to carry rifles. This is hardly unprecedented; Americans have eagerly fought for freedom throughout history. Most young people, however, could work in hospitals or daycare centers, guard our rail lines and transit systems, patrol our borders, monitor our seaports, guard power and chemical plants, help preserve national forests and waterways, or assist local, state and federal agencies that serve the nation's needs. If labor shortages developed in a given industry or geographical area,

some young people could work in essential private industries. Conscientious objectors could serve in non-combat roles. The handicapped could use their national service learning to handle their disabilities.

Again, the plan would enable the underprivileged to break out of ghettos and poverty-stricken areas, giving all young people an equal start. In effect, it would be like extending high school for another two years. It would be an opportunity, not a sacrifice. With well-organized young people, the program might even provide a way to tackle such problems as obesity, smoking and illicit drug use.

During the Holdenville High School graduation ceremony, senior Michael Lueking, Jr. wears his Marine uniform instead of the traditional cap and gown.

An Outline of Service

Military and intelligence authorities say the present war against terrorists is unlike any other in human history—no battle lines, no obvious targets. We aren't sure whom we're fighting. We are only told that the next terrorist attack may be against a national landmark, a vital industry or a down-home neighborhood. We're told that such an attack is a certainty. We can do nothing to stop it, but we can be ready for it.

In the 2001–2002 school year, more than 2.5 million students graduated from the nation's high schools. This is a manageable number. In the World War II years of 1942 and 1943 more than 6.3 million recruits were inducted into the U.S. military. These figures prove that the country is capable of training an enormous influx of potential talent. This reservoir of disciplined youngsters could be spread throughout the nation, poised to deal with any attack or disaster. Some could be dispatched to other lands, schooled in local languages and customs. They could be teachers and advisers, befriending overseas populations.

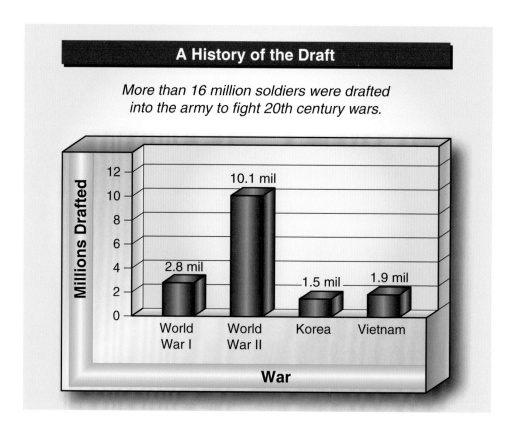

A History of the Draft

More than 16 million soldiers were drafted into the army to fight 20th century wars.

Under this plan, all high school graduates would go through a few weeks of "basic training" to establish discipline akin to that associated with the military. Afterwards, these trainees would fan out throughout the nation to undertake a wide variety of activities, and some undoubtedly would select combat training. Most would not. For example, many high school graduates emerge with two or three years of foreign language study. Under the discipline of national service, these youngsters could study their foreign languages more intensely, quickly becoming fluent. They then could be dispatched to other lands where translators are sorely needed. The president stated recently that the United States lags behind other nations in math and science. Under national service, kids who excelled in high school sciences could be given concentrated courses to prepare them to serve in government laboratories and eventually in scientific industries. Some educators say many high school graduates are not really ready for college or careers. A two-year break would be a chance to mature.

> ## American Troops Are Stretched Too Thin
>
> America's all-volunteer military simply cannot deploy and sustain enough troops to succeed in places like Iraq while still deterring threats elsewhere in the world.... The only effective solution to the manpower crunch is the one America has turned to again and again in its history: the draft.
>
> Phillip Carter and Paul Glastris, "The Case for the Draft," *Washington Monthly*, March 2005, pp. 19.

Following the Example of Other Nations

Organizing national service would be difficult. But surely the United States has enough brainpower in its colleges and universities to administer such a program, just as the military has done in the past wars. Again, mandatory national service has worked in other nations, so why not the United States? Would everyone embrace compulsory national service enthusiastically, or even willingly? Of course not. Some lawmakers would dissent. Some young people would rebel. National service would require the kind of leadership President John F. Kennedy exercised when he established the Peace Corps. Fifty-one nations have drafts, and Israel's is the toughest. Its men and women are subject to the draft at age 18. Men serve three years; women two years. Israelis then do one month of service per year until age 54. If other nations can do it, so can the U.S.

The Draft Will Save Money

A problem with past military drafts was that some individuals had enough clout to get deferments. Especially in the Vietnam War, many privileged persons stayed home while the underprivileged went into combat. That's why a period of national service must be universal—no exemptions for the sons and daughters of the well-connected. Everyone must go. It's likely that a "band-wagon" effect could prevail; youngsters might want to go because it's "the thing to do."

A two-year period of national service would, of course, be expensive, but not as costly as war. We're told that the wars in Afghanistan and Iraq, plus the Pentagon budget, amount to trillions of dollars, a sum beyond the comprehension of most Americans. So think of it this way: The U.S. is the most heavily indebted nation in the world, and much of this money is owed to China. If universal national service were adopted, some of this money might be recouped in the form of tangible benefits to the country.

When the U.S. draft was initiated on Oct. 29, 1940, more than a year before the Japanese attack on Pearl Harbor, the nation was woefully unprepared. Early recruits trained with broomsticks because they had no dries. Civilian vehicles wore signs saying "tank" because the army had too few real tanks. A period of universal national service now would guarantee that we'll never be that unprepared again.

We All Have an Obligation to Serve Our Country

A two-year break after high school is valuable, even without a crisis. This was proved after World War II when ex-servicemen and women invaded colleges to study under the GI Bill. These veterans were far more mature than kids fresh out of high school, and they excelled in earning degrees and

launching careers. Something akin to the GI Bill should be recreated. It is said to have produced America's most highly educated generation, and the payoff was an informed citizenry. So a period of universal national service would benefit individuals and the nation.

As President Kennedy put it "...ask what you can do for your country." Now is the time to do it.

Reinstating the draft may help the nation's young adults show pride in their country and themselves.

Analyze the Essay:

1. Walt Shotwell points to other nations that have the draft and says that if they can do it, so can the United States In your opinion, does the United States have the same military needs as other countries that require a draft? Explain your answer in order to argue for or against the reinstatement of the draft.

2. Shotwell makes a persuasive argument using examples and statistics, but he does not quote any experts or authorities to make his point, if you were to rewrite his essay, what kinds of voices might you include in the text, and where do you think the quotes should be placed in order to best support points being made?

The United States Should Not Reinstate the Draft

Winston Groom

In the following viewpoint author Winston Groom argues that reinstating the military draft is an impractical way to meet America's military needs. If all eligible men and women were really to be drafted, Groom points out, the military would be flooded with people needing training, supplies, and gear. The current military can barely meet these needs for its current enlistees, argues Groom, and thus is in no position to train and employ the more than 50 million people that would become eligible for service from a draft. Such a system would break America's budget, rendering it less capable of meeting military challenges. For these reasons Groom argues that reinstating the draft is not a viable solution for the United States Army.

Winston Groom is the author of *Forrest Gump* and fourteen other books, including four military histories.

Consider the Following Questions:

1. According to Groom, how many Americans would be eligible for a draft?
2. Why is a large military no longer necessary for today's military conflicts, according to the author?
3. What does the word "malcontents" mean in the context of the essay?

Winston Groom, "An Army of 50 Million? The Surpassingly Dishonest Draft Debate," *Weekly Standard*, vol. 12, December 11, 2006. Copyright © 2006, News America Incorporated, All Rights Reserved. Reproduced by permission.

Let's look at why so-called "universal military service" is a nutty idea: Presently there are about 50 million American men and women of draft age, between 18 and 28, with about 5 million more reaching draft age every year. (One must assume that women would be drafted equally with the men; in these times, how could they not be?) Now just ask yourselves: What on earth would the U.S. military do with all these people? They would all have to be housed, fed, clothed, transported, schooled, counseled, medically cared for—and you'd have to pay them something, wouldn't you? Otherwise they'd be slaves. Those costs alone would dwarf all the current entitlement programs in America.

A Draft Would Overwhelm the Military

And how could they even be trained and supplied? (At the very peak of World War II, the largest war in history, the U.S. military had about 16 million service men and women, and our relative taxes were higher than they had ever been.) And what about this: Presently there aren't nearly enough training tools—tanks and other military vehicles, planes, ships, artillery pieces, missiles, rifles and other weapons, communications devices, etc., let alone instructors—to possibly begin to instruct and equip all those millions of people in the armed forces.

So an additional taxpayer expense would, by necessity, be to multiply all of our present military bases (just when we're trying to get rid of as many of these dinosaurs as possible) as well as to multiply all the above-mentioned equipment by about 500 percent. And we would go positively broke doing it, just as the Russians did.

Draftees Would Have Nothing to Do

Even assuming this vast horde of 50 million—or let's just say half of that, 25 million, by the time you've weeded out people for one reason or another—were all uniformed, trained, and ready to go fight, the question then becomes: Where is it they would go, and with whom would they fight?

Fortunately, the threat of huge global land conflicts such as World War II, or some great war in Europe with the Soviet Union or in Asia against Communist China, has faded into oblivion. As it did, military planners tailored our fighting forces to the all-volunteer professional military we have today. Therefore, we would be left with this: Millions of newly drafted servicemen and women, languishing around U.S. bases, grousing about their two years of conscripted service, instead of being able to educate themselves or find useful and productive jobs.

[Rep. Charles] Rangel and his followers suggest that maybe those who didn't want to fight could be put in some

World War II required large military forces. More than 11 million Americans were drafted during that war.

sort of Civilian Service Corps. And what exactly would they do? Maybe they would come out and mow my lawn, but I doubt it.

Creating Inequities Among Americans

Possibly what these draft-renewal advocates have in mind, instead of the ridiculous notion of enlisting everybody of draft age, is some kind of return to the old end-of-the-Vietnam-war-era "draft lottery." Under this system, males (and now presumably females, too) upon reaching the age of 18 would each get a number and the highest numbers would be the only ones conscripted, as the military's needs dictated. But that would even be worse. To muster the 1.5 million active servicemen now on duty, you would only be conscripting about one percent of those draftees of eligible age. Some "universal service" that is!

And wouldn't those million or two young folks whose luck was to find themselves conscripted resent being dragooned into the military while the vast majority of their friends or classmates got the chance to go on with their lives and get ahead of them? What kind of soldiers, sailors, airmen, or Marines would they make? Especially since the two years of active duty Rangel is calling for would scarcely afford enough time to acquire the raw basics of the new and complicated military science.

Any way you look at it, if there is a renewed draft, the only fair and sensible way will be to go ahead and conscript everybody who is physically and mentally eligible. And then we, the American people, will be up to our eyeballs in superfluous and ineffectual military personnel at a stupendous and wasteful cost to the taxpayers—and to achieve what? Forced patriotism? Social engineering???

A Draft Would Lower the Quality of Soldiers

Modern warfare requires that even the most junior infantryman master a wide array of technical and tactical skills. Honing these skills to reflex, a prerequisite for survival in combat, takes time…. One- or two-year terms, the longest that would be likely under conscription, would simply not allow for this comprehensive training.

Nathaniel Fick, "Don't Dumb Down the Military," *New York Times,* July 20, 2004, p. A19.

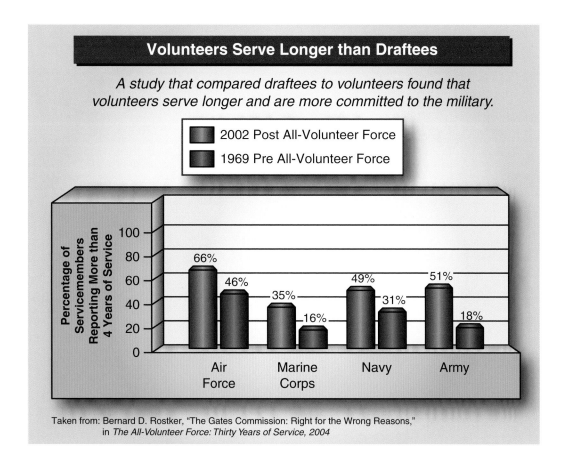

Volunteers Serve Longer than Draftees

A study that compared draftees to volunteers found that volunteers serve longer and are more committed to the military.

- ■ 2002 Post All-Volunteer Force
- ■ 1969 Pre All-Volunteer Force

Percentage of Servicemembers Reporting More than 4 Years of Service

Air Force: 66%, 46%
Marine Corps: 35%, 16%
Navy: 49%, 31%
Army: 51%, 18%

Taken from: Bernard D. Rostker, "The Gates Commission: Right for the Wrong Reasons," in *The All-Volunteer Force: Thirty Years of Service, 2004*

The U.S. military's mission has changed dramatically. I served as an officer in Vietnam, 1966–67, mostly with the First Brigade of the Fourth Infantry Division (the very same brigade that finally captured Saddam Hussein, I'm proud to say). But one thing I learned was that too many of the drafted soldiers did not perform as well as those who had volunteered. Quite a few of them didn't want to be there, and their attitudes showed it; a lot of them wound up in the stockade. Their hearts just weren't in it—and who could blame them? They would likely have fought hard and well in a "popular war" such as World War II, but Vietnam wasn't popular, and most felt they had been victims of the bad luck of the draw.

A Specialized Military Is a Better Military

What has happened since World War II, Korea, and Vietnam is that the military has become highly technical and specialized. The insides of a Vietnam-era tank looked pretty much like an enclosed bulldozer. Today, the insides of our main battle tank look like the control room of the Starship Enterprise, and it takes years of specialized training to work the thing properly. Same goes for the complicated machinery of "smart bombs," missiles, and electronics in the Navy and Air Force. And just about the time our new conscripts finally got the hang of it, their obligation would be up and we'd have to start all over again.

The American public apparently is not long willing to accept high battle casualties, and the only way to achieve this in modern combat is through the use of highly sophisticated weapons that take years to learn how to operate efficiently. Our present-day specialists are volunteers in an all-voluntary military. Many, if not most, expect to make a career out of it, and are willing to spend a good part of their lives to learn their trade. They don't want or need to be turned into anybody's political football. Not a single senior officer presently serving in the U.S. military thinks a return to the draft would be anything but a wasteful disaster.

Yes, if you begin drafting people into the armed forces again, you can probably train them to shoot a rifle, salute, march and drill, load an artillery piece, or swab the deck of a ship, just like in the old days. But the old days are gone. You won't get the dedication and special ability of the professionals we already have. What you will get instead is a gigantic, useless mob of half-trained malcontents whose skills are half-a-century outdated. The world already has too many militaries like that.

Analyze the Essay:

1. Winston Groom argues that the draft has the potential to cause inequities among Americans and "force patriotism" among the public. How do you think Walt Shotwell, author of the previous viewpoint, might respond to this claim?

2. In his essay, Shotwell suggested the draft should include a 2-year service requirement. What is Winston Groom's opinion of whether a 2-year period is appropriate for military service? With which author do you ultimately agree?

A Draft Would Make Military Service More Equal

William Broyles Jr.

In the following viewpoint, William Broyles, Jr. claims it is unfair that only certain sectors of the American population bear the burden of fighting wars. He explains how, increasingly, the military is made up of the poor and disadvantaged; the privileged rarely are the ones to do the fighting and dying in modern wars. Broyles points out that just a handful of politicians have children serving in the military, which is unfair considering they are the ones who make the decisions to go to war. Broyles suggests that a military draft would spread the burden of serving over all Americans. He concludes that if a war is really worth fighting, then all Americans should be willing to participate in it.

William Broyles, Jr. is the founding editor of *Texas Monthly*. His work has appeared in other publications, such as the *New York Times*, from which this viewpoint is taken.

Consider the Following Questions:

1. Who is Pat Tillman, and what point does Broyles make about him?
2. Who is the only member of Congress that has a child serving in the Iraq War, according to Broyles?
3. Who are the ultimate hypocrites, according to the author?

When my draft notice came in 1968, I was relieved in a way. Although I had deep doubts about the war, I had become troubled about how I had angled to avoid military service. My classmates from high school were in the war; my classmates from college were not—exactly the dynamic that exists today. But instead of reporting for service in the Army, on a whim I joined the Marine Corps, the last place on earth I thought I belonged.

Serving in the Military Changed Me

My sacrifice turned out to be minimal. I survived a year as an infantry lieutenant in Vietnam. I was not wounded; nor did I struggle for years with post-traumatic stress disorder. A long bout of survivor guilt was the price I paid. Others suffered far more, particularly those who had to serve after the war had lost all sense of purpose for the men fighting it. I like to think that in spite of my being so unwilling at first, I did some small service to my country and to that enduring love of mine, the United States Marine Corps.

To my profound surprise, the Marines did a far greater service to me. In three years I learned more about standards, commitment and yes, life, than I did in six years of university. I also learned that I had had no idea of my own limits: when I was exhausted after humping up and down jungle mountains in 100-degree heat with a 75-pound pack, terrified out of my mind, wanting only to quit, convinced I couldn't take another step, I found that in fact I could keep going for miles. And my life was put in the hands of young men I would otherwise never have met, by and large high-school dropouts, who turned out to be among the finest people I have ever known.

I am now the father of a young man who has far more character than I ever had. I joined the Marines because I had to; he signed up after college because he felt he ought to. He volunteered for an elite unit and has served in both Afghanistan and Iraq. When I see images of Americans in

A draft in today's society would benefit America if both men and women were enlisted into the military.

the war zones, I think of my son and his friends, many of whom I have come to know and deeply respect. When I opened this newspaper yesterday and read the front-page headline, "9 G.I.'s Killed," I didn't think in abstractions. I thought very personally.

A Burden Not Shared By Everyone

The problem is, I don't see the images of or read about any of the young men and women who, as [Vice President] Dick Cheney and I did, have "other priorities." There are no immediate family members of any of the prime civilian planners of this war serving in it—beginning with President [George W.] Bush and extending deep into the Defense Department. Only one of the 535 members of Congress, Senator Tim Johnson of South Dakota, has a child in the war—and only half a dozen others have sons and daughters in the military.

The memorial service yesterday for Pat Tillman, the football star killed in Afghanistan, further points out this contrast. He remains the only professional athlete of any sport who left his privileged life during this war and turned in his play uniform for a real one. With few exceptions, the only men and women in military service are the profoundly patriotic or the economically needy.

The Privileged Increasingly Don't Serve

It was not always so. In other wars, the men and women in charge made sure their family members led the way. Since 9/11, the war on terrorism has often been compared to the generational challenge of Pearl Harbor; but Franklin D. Roosevelt's sons all enlisted soon after that attack. Both of Lyndon B. Johnson's sons-in-law served in Vietnam.

This is less a matter of politics than privilege. The Democratic elites have not responded more nobly than have the Republican; it's just that the Democrats' hypocrisy is less acute. Our president's own family illustrates the loss of the sense of responsibility that once went with privilege. In three generations the Bushes have gone from war hero in World War II, to war evader in Vietnam, to none of the extended family showing up in Iraq and Afghanistan.

> ### The Burden of War Should Be Shared By All Income Brackets
>
> Right now, the only people being asked to sacrifice in any way are those men and women who, with limited options, chose military service and now find themselves in harm's way in Iraq. A draft would ensure that every economic group would have to do their share and not allow some to stay behind while other people's children do the fighting.
>
> Charles Rangel, "Rangel Reintroduces Draft Bill," Congressman Charles Rangel's web site, February 14, 2006. http://www.house.gov/list/press/ny15_rangel/CBRStatementonDraft0214200 6.html.

A War Fought By "Others"

Pat Tillman didn't want to be singled out for having done what other patriotic Americans his age should have done. The problem is, they aren't doing it. In spite of the president's insistence that our very civilization is at stake, the privileged aren't flocking to the flag. The war is being fought by Other

U.S. Military Recruits by Race

Military demographics tend to reflect America's demographics.
Most Americans serve in the military in relative proportion to the civilian population.

Race	Percent of 2004 U.S. Population	2004 Data				2005 Data			
		Percent of Recruits	Percent of Army	Recruit/ Population Ratio	Army/ Population Ratio	Percent of Recruits	Percent of Army	Recruit/ Population Ratio	Army/ Population Ratio
American Indian/Alaska Native	0.75%	2.01%	1.14%	2.68	1.52	2.62%	1.17%	3.49	1.56
Asian	4.23%	2.82%	2.39%	0.67	0.57	2.92%	2.07%	0.69	0.49
Black or African American	12.17%	14.54%	14.25%	1.19	1.17	12.99%	11.74%	1.07	0.96
Native Hawaiian or other Pacific Islander	0.14%	1.05%	0.93%	7.48	6.62	1.05%	0.90%	7.49	6.41
White	75.62%	73.12%	72.53%	0.97	0.96	73.12%	71.94%	0.97	0.95
Other	5.19%	---	---	---	---	---	---	---	---
Combination of two or more races	1.89%	1.52%	1.16%	0.80	0.61	0.93%	0.54%	0.18	0.10
Declined to respond	---	4.96%	7.61%	---	---	6.37%	11.64%	---	---

Taken from: Heritage Foundation calculations based on data from U.S. Department of Defense, Office of the Under Secretary of Defense for Personnel and Readiness, October 2002–September 2005 Non-Prior Service Active Duty Ascensions, and U.S. Census Bureau, 2004 American Community Survey, Table B02001.

People's Children. The war is impersonal for the very people to whom it should be most personal.

If the children of the nation's elites were facing enemy fire without body armor, riding through gantlets of bombs in unarmored Humvees, fighting desperately in an increasingly hostile environment because of arrogant and incompetent civilian leadership, then those problems might well find faster solutions.

The men and women on active duty today—and their companions in the National Guard and the reserves—have seen their willingness, and that of their families, to make sacrifices for their country stretched thin and finally abused. Thousands of soldiers promised a one-year tour of duty have seen that promise turned into a lie. When Eric Shinseki, then the Army chief of staff, told the president that winning the war and peace in Iraq would take hundreds of thousands more troops, Mr. Bush ended his career. As a result of this and other ill-advised decisions, the war is in danger of being lost, and my beloved military is being run into the ground.

Congressman Charles Rangel, shown here, has argued that the draft should be reinstated so that all classes and races share America's military burden equally.

The Voluntary Military Is Abused

This abuse of the voluntary military cannot continue. How to ensure adequate troop levels, with a diversity of backgrounds? How to require the privileged to shoulder their fair share? In other words, how to get today's equivalents of Bill Clinton, George W. Bush, Dick Cheney—and me—into the military, where their talents could strengthen and revive our fighting forces?

The only solution is to bring back the draft. Not since the 19th century has America fought a war that lasted longer than a week with an all-volunteer army; we can't do it now. It is simply not built for a protracted major conflict. The arguments against the draft—that a voluntary army is of higher quality, that the elites will still find a way to evade service—are bogus. In World War II we used a draft army to fight the Germans and Japanese—two of the most powerful military machines in history—and we won. The problems in the military toward the end of Vietnam were not caused by the draft; they were the result of young Americans being sent to fight and die in a war that had become a disaster.

To Not Fight Is to Be a Hypocrite

One of the few good legacies of Vietnam is that after years of abuses we finally learned how to run the draft fairly. A strictly impartial lottery, with no deferments, can ensure that the draft intake matches military needs. Chance, not connections or clever manipulation, would determine who serves.

If this war is truly worth fighting, then the burdens of doing so should fall on all Americans. If you support this war, but assume that Pat Tillman and Other People's Children should fight it, then you are worse than a hypocrite. If it's not worth your family fighting it, then it's not worth it, period. The draft is the truest test of public support for the administration's handling of the war, which is perhaps why the administration is so dead set against bringing it back.

Analyze the Essay:

1. Broyles begins his essay be recounting his experience in the military during the Vietnam War. What did these comments lend to the rest of the essay? Did you think this was an effective way to begin? Explain your answer.
2. Broyles argues that the majority of people who make up the all-volunteer military are poor or minorities. How does Fred Kaplan, author of the following viewpoint, respond to this claim?

A Draft Would Not Make Military Service More Equal

Fred Kaplan

In the following viewpoint, Fred Kaplan argues that the draft would not improve the current state of the military. First, he counters claims that minorities and the poor disproportionately serve in the military; the military is more diverse than it used to be, he argues, and minorities serve in general proportion to their numbers in society. Secondly, Kaplan sees no guarantee that a draft would make the poor and rich serve equally—like in Vietnam, he argues, the elite will find ways to dodge the draft. Finally, Kaplan argues a draft would lower the quality of those who serve in the military and make it impossible to adequately train so many forces. For these reason he believes it is not appropriate to reinstate the draft.

Fred Kaplan writes the "War Stories" column for *Slate. com,* an online magazine from which this viewpoint was taken.

Consider the Following Questions:

1. According to Kaplan, what percent of military recruits are African-American?
2. At what level does the average military recruit read, according to the author?
3. Why would a draft not guarantee that everyone would serve equally, in Kaplan's opinion?

It's a complex business, calculating how many troops a nation needs. No matter how you do the math, though, one thing is clear: The United States doesn't have enough.

Should we, must we, bring back the draft to fill the gaps? . . .

Rep. Charles Rangel, the political leader of Harlem and the dean of New York's Democratic congressional delegation, is proposing a revival of the draft, in part to address precisely this issue of social justice—"to make it clear," as he said last year, "that if there were a war, there would be more equitable representation of people making sacrifices." Rangel, who fought in the Korean War, added, with a twist of the knife, "Those who love this country have a patriotic obligation to defend this country. For those who say the poor fight better, I say give the rich a chance."

Rangel had a second motive for bringing back the draft—to reduce the likelihood of military adventures in the first place. "I truly believe," he said, "that those who make the decision and those who support the United States going into war would feel more readily the pain that's involved, the sacrifice that's involved, if they thought that the fighting force would include the affluent and those who historically have avoided this great responsibility."

It has been widely noted that only one U.S. senator has had a son fighting in Iraq. Might more lawmakers have been more hesitant to vote for that war had their sons and daughters been eligible for call-up?

Rangel's premises have some validity, but not as much as he apparently thinks.

For one thing, today's all-volunteer American military is not nearly as poor or as black as it once was.

In 2002 (the most recent year for which official data have been compiled), 182,000 people enlisted in the U.S. military. Of these recruits, 16 percent were African-American. By comparison, blacks constituted 14 percent of 18-to-24-year-olds in the U.S. population overall. In other words, black young men and women are only slightly over-represented among new enlistees. Hispanics, for their part, are

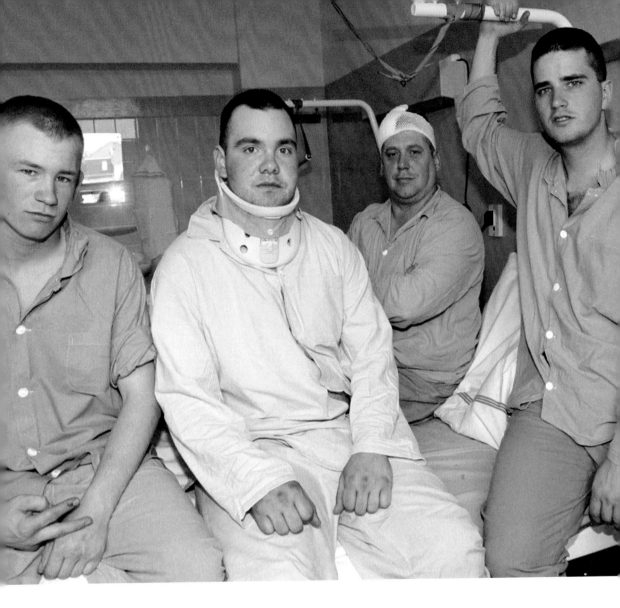

under-represented, comprising just 11 percent of recruits, compared with 16 percent of 18-to-24-year-olds.

Looking at the military as a whole, not just at those who signed up in a single year, blacks do represent a disproportionate share—22 percent of all U.S. armed forces. By comparison, they make up 13 percent of 18-to-44-year-old civilians. The difference is that blacks re-enlist at a higher rate than whites. (Hispanics remain under-represented:

How the draft might affect the race and gender of soldiers is of considerable debate.

Household Income of U.S. Military Recruits

Military Recruits Are Not The Poorest Americans

Median Household Income Range	Percent of U.S. Population, Ages 18–24	Percent of 2003 Recruits	Percent of 2004 Recruits	Percent of 2005 Recruits	2003 Difference	2004 Difference	2005 Difference
$0–$29,375	19.79%	14.61%	14.14%	13.66%	-5.18%	-5.65%	-6.13%
$29,382–$35,462	20.04%	19.56%	19.24%	19.21%	-0.49%	-0.81%	-0.83%
$35,463–$41,685	20.05%	21.15%	21.21%	21.46%	1.09%	1.15%	1.41%
$41,688–$52,068	20.10%	22.52%	22.70%	22.82%	2.42%	2.60%	2.72%
$52,071–$200,001	20.02%	22.17%	22.72%	22.85%	2.15%	2.70%	2.83%

Taken from: Heritage Foundation calculations based on data from U.S. Department of Defense, Office of the Under Secretary of Defense for Personnel and Readiness, October 2002–September 2005 Non-Prior Service Active Duty Ascensions, and U.S. Census Bureau, *United States Census 2000*, Summary, File 3.

10 percent of all armed forces, as opposed to 14 percent of 18-to-44-year-old civilians.)

Still, the military's racial mix is more diverse than it used to be. In 1981, African-Americans made up 33 percent of the armed forces. So, over the past two decades, their share has diminished by one-third. This decline began in the mid-'80s, when the military decided no longer to accept re-enlistments from soldiers who scored low on the aptitude test.

As a result, the scores have risen since the '80s. More than that, the aptitude of U.S. military personnel now exceeds that of American civilians. . . .

Other indicators confirm this impression. The average recruit has an 11th-grade reading level; the average civilian can read at a 10th-grade level. Nearly all recruits—97 percent of female, 94 percent of male—graduated from high school; 79 percent of civilians have high-school diplo-

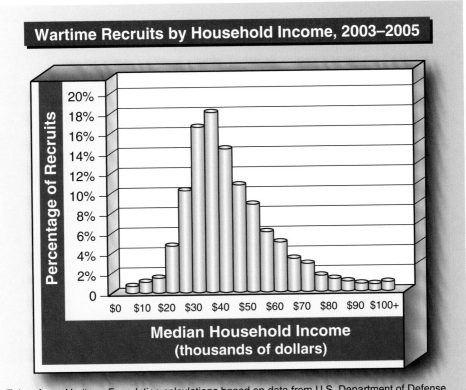

Wartime Recruits by Household Income, 2003–2005

Percentage of Recruits

20%
18%
16%
14%
12%
10%
8%
6%
4%
2%
0

$0 $10 $20 $30 $40 $50 $60 $70 $80 $90 $100+

Median Household Income
(thousands of dollars)

Taken from: Heritage Foundation calculations based on data from U.S. Department of Defense, Office of the Under Secretary of Defense for Personnel and Readiness, October 2002–September 2005 Non-Prior Service Active Duty Ascensions, and U.S. Census Bureau, *United States Census 2000*, Summary, File 3

mas. Officers are better-educated still: All are now required to have college degrees.

In short, today's armed forces are not the downtrodden, ethnically lopsided social rejects that they tended to be after the Vietnam War, when the all-volunteer military came into being.

Bringing back the draft would lasso the social dregs along with the society elite. Would the net effect be a "more equitable representation of people making sacrifices," as Rangel put it? Maybe, maybe not. Even with a draft, not everyone would serve. About 11 million Americans are 20 to 26 years old. The military doesn't need 11 million people. A draft would have to involve some sort of lottery. If that's the way

The country's leaders face the question of whether reinstating the draft would be appropriate in today's society.

it goes, there should be no exemptions (except for the physically disabled, the mentally incompetent, convicted felons, and perhaps conscientious objectors). Still, unless a military draft was one component of a compulsory national-service program (the subject of another essay), only some would be called. It's a matter of chance whether the kids from the suburbs would be called more than the kids from the projects.

There is a still more basic question: What is the purpose of a military? Is it to spread the social burden—or to fight and win wars? The U.S. active-duty armed forces are more professional and disciplined than at any time in decades, perhaps ever. This is so because they are composed of people who passed comparatively stringent entrance exams—and, more important, people who want to be there or, if they no longer want to be there, know that they chose to be there in the first place. An Army of draftees would include many bright, capable, dedicated people; but it would also include many dumb, incompetent malcontents, who would wind up getting more of their fellow soldiers killed.

It takes about six months to put a soldier through basic training. It takes a few months more to train one for a specialized skill. The kinds of conflicts American soldiers are likely to face in the coming decades will be the kinds of conflicts they are facing in Iraq, Afghanistan, Kosovo, and Bosnia—"security and stabilization operations," in military parlance. These kinds of operations require more training—and more delicate training—than firing a rifle, driving a tank, or dropping a bomb.

If conscription is revived, draftees are not likely to serve more than two years. Right now, the average volunteer in the U.S. armed forces has served five years. By most measures, an Army of draftees would be less experienced, less cohesive—generally, less effective—than an Army of volunteers. Their task is too vital to tolerate such a sacrifice for the cause of social justice, especially when that cause isn't so urgent to begin with.

> ## The Weight of Service Is Equally Shared
>
> With regard to income, education, race, and regional background, the all-volunteer force is representative of our nation and meets standards set by Congress and the Department of Defense. ... No evidence supports arguments for reinstating the draft or altering recruiting policies to achieve more equitable representation.
>
> Tim Kane, "Who Are the Recruits?" Heritage Foundation, October 26, 2006, p. 12. www.heritage.org/Research/NationalSecurity/cda05-08.cfm.

Would lawmakers be less likely to approve and fund wars if their children and the children of their friends might be drafted to fight? The answer is unclear. The one senator whose son fought in Iraq, Sen. Tim Johnson, Dem-S.D., voted for the war resolution and all subsequent funding measures. True, the senator's son, who was serving in the 101st Airborne Division, did volunteer; Johnson's vote could be seen as a token of support for his son. Would other senators vote differently? If patriotism or party loyalty did not play a role, might they fear accusations of selfishness or cowardice if they seemed to oppose a war simply to save their children's hides?

Nonetheless, we do need more troops. How do we get them, if not from a draft? The inescapable answer is that we have to pay more for them, maybe a lot more. Those of us who do not volunteer enjoy more freedom, leisure, and in many cases income, as a result. It is not asking too much to sacrifice some of that extra income for those who risk the ultimate sacrifice.

Educational Level of U.S. Military Recruits

Educational Level	2003 Recruits	2004 Recruits	2005 Recruits	2004 Population
No high school credentials	1.85%	1.85%	1.95%	
High school senior	1.37%	1.37%	1.33%	20.20%
General Equivalency Diploma	7.03%	7.03%	9.40%	
High school diploma graduate	82.66%	82.66%	80.43%	33.80%
Associate's degree	1.23%	1.23%	1.26%	
Greater than high school credentials	5.87%	5.87%	5.63%	46.00%
High school graduation rate	96.78%	96.78%	96.72%	79.80%

Sources: Heritage Foundation calculations based on data from U.S. Department of Defense, Office of the Under Secretary of Defense for Personnel and Readiness, October 2002–September 2005 Non-Prior Service Active Duty Accessions, and U.S. Census Bureau, 2004 American Community Survey. Table S1501, at factfinder.census.gov/servlet/STTable?_bm = y&- geo_id = 01000US&-qr_name = ACS_2004_EST_G00_S1501&-ds_name = ACS_2004_EST_G00_(August 9, 2006).

Analyze the Essay:

1. Although Fred Kaplan opposes a draft, he acknowledges that more troops are needed in order to improve the military. What alternative to the draft does he suggest? What is your opinion of this plan?

2. Fred Kaplan argues that the draft will not make the military more diverse or equal. The author of the previous viewpoint, William Broyles, Jr., disagrees. After reading both viewpoints, which author do you think is right? Explain your answer using evidence from the texts you have read.

A Draft Would Improve the Character of Americans

Armstrong Williams

Armstrong Williams has a widely syndicated newspaper column, radio talk show and television program, and is one of the leading conservative African American voices in the country. In the following viewpoint, Williams argues that instituting a military draft could improve the character of Americans. Military service, in Williams' view, would teach young people to respect their nation and work together towards a common goal, which in turn would lead to a drop in crime, vandalism, and other problems that plague American neighborhoods. Furthermore, conscription would give all Americans valuable skills and expose them to new technology, which would allow America to reassert itself in the global marketplace as a leader in technology and innovation. Williams concludes that a draft not only would help America meet its defense needs but positively affect the character of its citizens.

Consider the Following Questions:

1. What are some features of the conscription plan that Williams proposes?
2. What affect would being drafted have on troubled teens, according to the author?
3. What types of skills does Williams say a conscript should learn in the military?

Armstong Williams, "The U.S. Needs Mandatory Military Service," *Afro-American Red Star (Washington DC)*, vol. 114, June 24–30, 2006, p. A11. Copyright © 2006 Afro-American Newspapers. Reproduced by permission.

Would you like to see your son, daughter, niece, nephew or teenage neighbor become hard-working, respectful, disciplined, honorable and prepared for life? Would you like to see crime, teenage pregnancy and substance abuse rates decline? No, this is not an advertisement for a magic pill; this is an argument for mandatory military service.

Discipline, national pride, and a strong work ethic are some of the qualities serving in the military can instill in young people.

Instill Honorable Qualities into Our Society

Each passing generation produces teenagers who are more and more brazen, disrespectful, lazy and ill-qualified for success in the real world. Thus, our society becomes more dangerous, depleted and dishonest every year. With one simple—albeit radical—move, our government could eliminate these problems and help our children and our country reach its potential. Mandatory military service, or conscription, could cure many of our societal ills and allow American teenagers to truly reach their potential.

Mandatory military service is one of the oldest forms of national service and is common to both democratic and non-democratic countries. Such democratic countries as Austria, Brazil, Denmark, Finland, Germany, Israel, Mexico, Norway, Russia, South Korea, Sweden, Switzerland and Turkey require male and occasionally female citizens to participate in military service when they become 18 years old. These countries prove that conscription, when handled properly, can be an asset to the military, the society and the conscript.

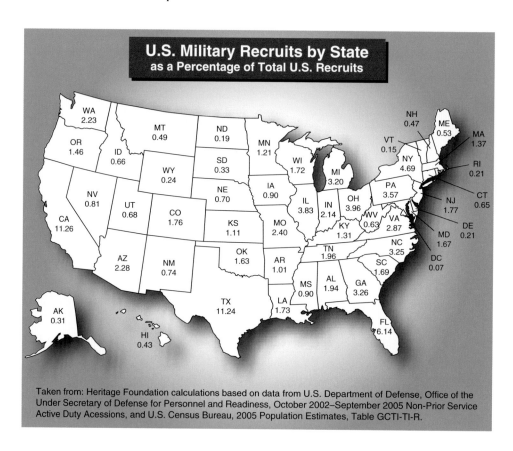

U.S. Military Recruits by State
as a Percentage of Total U.S. Recruits

WA 2.23
OR 1.46
MT 0.49
ND 0.19
MN 1.21
NH 0.47
ME 0.53
MA 1.37
VT 0.15
ID 0.66
WY 0.24
SD 0.33
WI 1.72
MI 3.20
NY 4.69
RI 0.21
NV 0.81
UT 0.68
CO 1.76
NE 0.70
IA 0.90
IL 3.83
IN 2.14
OH 3.96
PA 3.57
NJ 1.77
CT 0.65
CA 11.26
KS 1.11
MO 2.40
KY 1.31
WV 0.63
VA 2.87
DE 0.21
MD 1.67
AZ 2.28
NM 0.74
OK 1.63
AR 1.01
TN 1.96
NC 3.25
DC 0.07
SC 1.69
TX 11.24
LA 1.73
MS 0.90
AL 1.94
GA 3.26
FL 6.14
AK 0.31
HI 0.43

Taken from: Heritage Foundation calculations based on data from U.S. Department of Defense, Office of the Under Secretary of Defense for Personnel and Readiness, October 2002–September 2005 Non-Prior Service Active Duty Acessions, and U.S. Census Bureau, 2005 Population Estimates, Table GCTI-TI-R.

A Plan for Conscription

Here's my basic plan for American conscription: Every able-bodied citizen (both men and women) must honorably serve at least two years in the United States military before they are 25 years old. They can enter the military branch of their liking, request to be trained in a specific field and serve in the state of their choice. Furthermore, the military will guarantee that conscience objectors or conscripts wary of conflict will be placed only in non-hostile positions. After two years of service, conscripts are free to depart the military if they choose to do so.

Mandatory military service benefits the military, the country and the conscript. The military benefits because their forces increase dramatically. For a small increase in expenses, they receive an influx of able young men and women—including many of the best and brightest, who often avoid joining a professional army. Resources that go into recruiting programs can be used toward training and, because of higher head counts, outsourcing and subcontracting jobs can more easily be handled in house.

A Draft Can Make Society More Charitable

A compulsory national service program would give our youth—and future leaders—a shaping civic experience. The revival of the citizen soldier can only be to the advantage of the armed services and the nation.

Charles Moskos, "Feel that Draft?" *Chicago Tribune*, June 8, 2005, p. 23..

The United States benefits from conscription because national spirit increases, national unity improves, neighborhoods become safer and society grows healthier.

All Corners of Society Would Benefit

With conscription, troubled teens who normally head to street corners enter the military and receive the training, discipline and experience that propel them to a stable and secure life. They unite with people of all sexes, races and religions to work toward a common good. This allows neighborhoods to become safer and society to become stron-

ger. The workforce gets better workers, families get better mothers and fathers, and the country gets a more unified citizenship.

The conscript benefits from military service because they learn practical life skills such as first aid, wilderness survival, computer proficiency and self-defense. They become physically fit, mentally strong and knowledgeable in multiple areas. Conscripts learn how to work hard, discipline themselves, follow orders, think on their feet and lead their peers. Most importantly, they come away from the military with skills that benefit society, the workplace and the family. With a college degree, the men and women who served their two years with honors will be sought after by the public and private sectors.

Answering the Critics

Of course there are many people who believe conscription armies are illegal, immoral and ineffective. Arguments have been made (and sometimes history has shown) that conscripts often have low morale, little motivation and a lack of displace to properly serve in the armed forces.

Some say that many conscripts are physically or mentally unfit to be trusted and need training, educating and counseling that the military cannot provide. And finally, because of time and resource constrictions, many mandatory military service opponents point out that conscripts usually only receive rudimentary training which can cause bloodshed during hostile situations. Besides these noted disadvantages, some economists believe that conscription armies cost more than voluntary ones. These disadvantages are certainly valid, and I welcome them in a debate about conscription.

Mandatory military service may seem too drastic, too un-American or too impractical to implement in the 21st century, but it is a legitimate idea that deserves a fair discussion and open debate.

A review of current democracies using conscription, an analysis of the U.S. military and an evaluation of our country's civilian state leads me to believe that conscription is the answer to many of our country's—and children's—woes.

Analyze the Essay:

1. Williams acknowledges that there are valid complaints about forcing people to serve in the military. What are these complaints, and how does Williams incorporate them into his pro-draft essay?
2. Armstrong Williams and Katha Pollitt, author of the following viewpoint, disagree on what effect reinstating the draft would have on American society. After reading both viewpoints, with which author do you agree? Cite evidence from the text in your answer.

A Draft Would Militarize American Society

Katha Pollitt

In the following viewpoint, Katha Pollitt argues against reinstating the draft because it would result in a militarized society. A more militarized nation would be more prone to violence and war, she suggests, and ultimately spend more money for defense than it does presently. With a larger military force, Pollitt also believes there would be a greater likelihood of military actions undertaken, increasing the number of wars in the world. She contends that any perceived benefits, such as a more diverse or equitable military, would not be worth the price to society.

Katha Pollitt is an author and longtime columnist for *The Nation*, from which this viewpoint was taken.

Consider the Following Questions:

1. Why does Pollitt not believe that the draft will encourage Americans to sacrifice for the military?
2. Why does the author believe that bringing back the draft will not strengthen antiwar sentiment, as some argue?
3. According to the author, what might be the economic consequences of a renewed draft?

Katha Pollitt, "Do You Feel a Draft?" *Nation*, vol. 278, June 7, 2004, p. 9. Copyright © 2004 by The Nation Magazine/The Nation Company, Inc. Reproduced by permission.

Should the government bring back the draft? Republican Senator Chuck Hagel has been talking it up, and it has captured the imagination of many liberals and leftists as well. [In 2003] antiwar Representative Charles Rangel of New York and Senator Fritz Hollings of South Carolina introduced proposals to restore the draft as a way to build opposition to the war: The draft, Rangel argued, would spread the burden of war throughout society and force war supporters in the upper classes to put their children where their mouths are.

Arguments Against the Draft

On paper, it's a tempting argument. Universal conscription would certainly be a poke in the eye for Bush, Cheney, Wolfowitz, Feith, Perle and other prowar "chickenhawks" who used their social privilege to avoid Vietnam ("I had other priorities," said the Vice President, who enjoyed no fewer than five deferments). In theory, the draft would give us an army of "citizen soldiers," young men—and probably women—drawn from all parts of society, instead of the current Army, which draws heavily on military families, poor people and—to judge by Charles Graner, accepted into the Army in his early 30s despite a long history of violence and instability—wife-beating losers. For many, the draft summons up ideals of valor, adulthood, public service and self-sacrifice—*shared* self-sacrifice. Those are all good things, but the draft is still a bad idea.

Given our ever more stratified and atomized society, why expect the draft to be equal or fair? In the 1960s, the draft was famously open to evasion and manipulation, as that large flock of chickenhawks proves. The new draft would be too. The Army doesn't need every high school graduate—there are 612,836 men 18 to 26 in the Selective Service registry for the state of Ohio alone, more than four times the number of US soldiers in Iraq—so it will be able, as in the past, to pick and choose. When one loophole closes, another will open: If Rangel succeeds in banning student deferments, we'll see 4Fs for college-bound kids with "attention deficit disorder" or "learning disabilities." Privileged kids will be funneled into safe stateside units, just the way George W. Bush was.

Conscription Will Increase Militarism

What about the argument that the draft will produce opposition to war? ("Parents and children would suddenly care," as historian of the 1960s Jon Wiener told me.) It's true that the draft will make it harder for kids and their families to live in a golden bubble—in the l960s, the draft concentrated the minds of college students wonderfully well. But mostly what the Vietnam-era draft produced was the abolition of the draft: That was the immediate form that opposition to the war took for those who most risked having to fight it. Abolishing the draft was a tremendous victory for the antiwar movement. If draftees were used in an unpopular war tomorrow, wouldn't opponents demand that kids not be forced to kill and be killed in an unjust and pointless cause? Nor is it entirely clear that a draft would raise antiwar sentiment overall. Conscription might make it harder, not easier, for many people to see a war's wrongness: It's hard to admit your children died in vain.

Supporters of the draft are using it to promote indirectly politics we should champion openly and up front. It's terrible that working-class teenagers join the Army to get college funds, or job training, or work—what kind of nation is this where Jessica Lynch had to invade Iraq in order to

> **The Madness of War**
>
> If you, as a young adult, are conscripted into military service, ask yourself this question: would it be better for me to appease my country by choosing to kill others in the name of a coin-engraved, cookie-cutter, American-sized God, or might it be more appropriate, more noble even, to choose to be and advocate for life by having the courage to say yes to humanity and not to the draft, by having the guts to make a determined stand against the God awful madness of war?
>
> Doug Soderstrom, "A Reinstated Military Draft? Advice from an Old Man," *CommonDreams*, January 9, 2006. www.commondreams.org.

Many Americans worry that reinstating the draft in the United States would lead to a more violent and militarized society.

fulfill her modest dream of becoming an elementary school teacher and Shoshanna Johnson had to be a cook on the battlefield to qualify for a culinary job back home? But the solution isn't to force more people into the Army, it's affordable education and good jobs for all. Nobody should have to choose between risking her life—or as we see in Abu Ghraib, her soul—and stocking shelves at Wal-Mart. By the same token, threatening our young with injury, madness and death is a rather roundabout way to increase resistance to military adventures. I'd rather just loudly insist that people who favor war go fight in it themselves or be damned as weasels and shirkers. I'm sure the Army can find something for Christopher Hitchens to do.

More Violence, Not Less

The main effect of bringing back the draft would be to further militarize the nation. The military has already thrust its tentacles deep into civilian life: We have ROTC [Reserve Officers' Training Corps] on campus, Junior ROTC in the high schools, Hummers in our garages and camouflage couture in our closets. Whole counties, entire professions, live or die by defense contracts—which is perhaps one reason we spend more on our military budget than the next twenty-five countries combined. (Did you know that the money raised by the breast cancer postage stamp goes to the Defense Department?) Conscription will make the country more authoritarian and probably more violent, too, if that's possible—especially for women soldiers, who are raped and assaulted in great numbers in today's armed forces, usually with more or less impunity.

If we want a society that is equal, cohesive, fair and war-resistant, let's fight for that, not punish our children for what we have allowed America to become.

Analyze the Essay:

1. Pollitt argues that a draft will cause society to put an emphasis on war, not on making the military more equitable. How do you think authors such as William Broyles Jr. and Armstrong Williams would respond to this claim?

2. Pollitt believes that involving more people in the military will make the nation more prone to violence and militaristic behavior. What is your opinion of this claim? What evidence does the author use to support it? After analyzing her argument, state whether or not you agree with her.

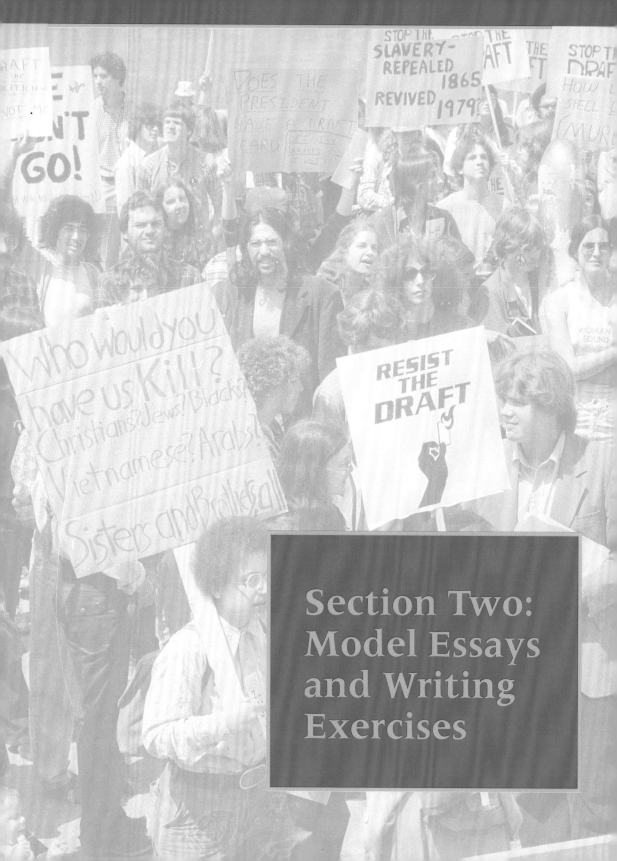

Section Two:
Model Essays
and Writing
Exercises

The Five-Paragraph Essay

An *essay* is a short piece of writing that discusses or analyzes one topic. The five-paragraph essay is a form commonly used in school assignments and tests. Every five-paragraph essay begins with an *introduction,* ends with a *conclusion,* and features three *supporting paragraphs* in the middle.

The Thesis Statement. The introduction includes the essay's thesis statement. The thesis statement presents the argument or point the author is trying to make about the topic. The essays in this book all have different thesis statements because they are making different arguments about the military draft.

The thesis statement should clearly tell the reader what the essay will be about. A focused thesis statement helps determine what will be in the essay; the subsequent paragraphs are spent developing and supporting its argument.

The Introduction. In addition to presenting the thesis statement, a well-written introductory paragraph captures the attention of the reader and explains why the topic being explored is important. It may provide the reader with background information on the subject matter or feature an anecdote that illustrates a point relevant to the topic. It could also present startling information that clarifies the point of the essay or put forth a contradictory position that the essay will refute. Further techniques for writing an introduction are found later in this section.

The Supporting Paragraphs. The introduction is then followed by three (or more) supporting paragraphs. These are the main body of the essay. Each paragraph presents and develops a subtopic that supports the essay's thesis statement. Each *subtopic* is spearheaded by a *topic sentence* and supported by its own facts, details, and examples. The writer can use various kinds of supporting material and details to back up the topic of each supporting paragraph. These may include statistics, quotations from people with special knowledge or expertise, historic facts, and anecdotes. A rule of writing is that specific and concrete examples are more convincing than vague, general, or unsupported assertions.

The Conclusion. The conclusion is the paragraph that closes the essay. Its function is to summarize or reiterate the main idea of the essay. It may recall an idea from the introduction or briefly examine the larger implications of the thesis. Because the conclusion is also the last chance a writer has to make an impression on the reader, it is important that it not simply repeat what has been presented elsewhere in the essay but close it in a clear, final, and memorable way.

Although the order of the essay's component paragraphs is important, they do not have to be written in the order presented here. Some writers like to decide on a thesis and write the introduction paragraph first. Other writers like to focus first on the body of the essay, and write the introduction and conclusion later.

Pitfalls to Avoid

When writing essays about controversial issues such as the military draft, it is important to remember that disputes over the material are common precisely because there are many different perspectives. Remember to state your arguments in careful and measured terms. Evaluate your topic fairly—avoid overstating negative qualities of one perspective or understating positive qualities of another. Use examples, facts, and details to support any assertions you make.

The Persuasive Essay

There are many types of essays, but in general, they are usually short compositions in which the writer expresses and discusses an opinion about something. In the persuasive essay the writer tries to persuade (convince) the reader to do something or to agree with the writer's opinion about something. Examples of persuasive writing are easy to find. Advertising is one common example. Through commercial and print ads, companies try to convince the public to buy their products for specific reasons. Much everyday writing is persuasive, too. Letters to the editor, posts from sports fans on team Web sites, even handwritten notes urging a friend to listen to a new CD—all are examples of persuasive writing.

The Tools of Persuasion

The writer of the persuasive essay uses various tools to persuade the reader. Here are some of them:

- *Facts and statistics.* A fact is a statement that no one, typically, would disagree with. It can be verified by information in reputable resources, such as encyclopedias, almanacs, government Web sites, or reference books about the topic of the fact.

Examples of Facts and Statistics

Americans celebrate their nation's birth every Fourth of July.

Sacramento is the capital of California.

The average American eats 252 eggs each year.

A 2005 survey by the Science Museum in London found that 1 in 15 people have reported seeing a UFO.

It is important to note that facts and statistics can be *misstated* (written down or quoted incorrectly), *misinterpreted* (not understood correctly by the user), or *misused* (not used fairly). But, if a writer uses facts and statistics properly, they can add authority to the writer's essay.

- *Opinions.* An opinion is what a person thinks about something. It can be contested or argued with. However, opinions of people who are experts on the topic or who have personal experience are often very convincing. Many persuasive essays are written to convince the reader that the writer's opinion is worth believing and acting on.
- *Testimonials.* A testimonial is a statement given by a person who is thought to be an expert or who has another trait people admire, such as being a celebrity. Television commercials frequently use testimonials to convince watchers to buy the products they are advertising.
- *Examples and anecdotes.* An example is something that is representative of a group or type ("red" is an example of the group "color"). Examples are used to help define, describe, or illustrate something to make it more understandable. Anecdotes are extended examples. They are little stories with a beginning, middle, and end. They can be used just like examples to explain something or to show something about a topic.
- *Appeals to reason.* One way to convince readers that an opinion or action is right is to appeal to reason or logic. This often involves the idea that if some ideas are true, another must also be true. Here is an example of one type of appeal to reason:

The Humane Society rescues many animals every year. The Humane Society needs money to keep operating. Therefore, if you love animals, you should contribute money to the Humane Society.

- *Appeals to emotion.* Another way to persuade readers to believe or do something is to appeal to their emotions—love, fear, pity, loyalty, and anger are some of the emotions to which writers appeal. A writer who wants to persuade the reader that Americans should be drafted into the military might appeal to the reader's sense of loyalty ("Every American must equally share the responsibility of protecting this nation—we cannot let only the bravest and most responsible members of society carry this heavy burden that benefits us all.")
- *Ridicule and name-calling.* Ridicule and name-calling are not good techniques to use in a persuasive essay. Instead of exploring the strengths of the topic, the writer who uses these relies on making those who oppose the main idea look foolish, evil, or stupid. In most cases, the writer who does this weakens the argument.
- *Bandwagon.* The writer who uses the bandwagon technique uses the idea that "Everybody thinks this or is doing this; therefore it is valid." The bandwagon method is not a very authoritative way to convince your reader of your point.

Words and Phrases Common to Persuasive Essays

accordingly
because
consequently
clearly
for this reason
this is why
indeed
it is necessary to
it makes sense to
it seems clear that
it stands to reason
it then follows that
obviously
since
subsequently
therefore
thus
we must

Students Should Never Be Drafted Into the Military

Editor's Notes The first model essay argues that students should never be drafted into the military. The author explains why she believes students do not make good soldiers, and tries to convince the reader to agree with her. The essay is structured as a five-paragraph essay in which each paragraph contributes a supporting piece of evidence to develop the argument.

The notes in the margin point out key features of the essay, and will help you understand how the essay is organized. Also note that all sources are cited using Modern Language Association (MLA) style. For more information on how to cite your sources see Appendix C. In addition, consider the following:

- How does the introduction engage the reader's attention?
- What persuasive techniques are used in the essay?
- What purpose do the essay's quotes serve?
- Does the essay convince you of its point?

Refers to thesis and topic sentences

Refers to supporting details

Paragraph 1

At the height of the opposition to the Vietnam War, students across the nation united their voices in saying no to both the war and the draft, which randomly selected men as young as 19 years old to serve in the military whether they wanted to or not. Increasing opposition to the morality of the war, as well as complaints that the draft was easy for the privileged to dodge or serve in partial capacity, led thousands of young students eligible for conscription to burn their draft cards or

The introduction is meant to pique your interest in the topic and draw you into the essay. Does it accomplish this?

Editor's Note: In applying MLA style guidelines in this book, the following simplifications have been made: Parenthetical text citations are confined to direct quotations only; electronic source documentation in the Works Cited list omits date of access, page ranges, and some detailed facts of publication.

flee to Canada. As a result of their efforts, the draft was discontinued in 1973. Today, discussions of reinstating the draft to meet the challenges of the War on Terror are increasingly heard, but Americans must resist the temptation to send the nation's youngest, most promising resource off to war.

Paragraph 2

It is commonly argued that those old enough to fight in a war should be allowed to legally drink alcohol, but the reverse is also true. Students are young, impressionable, and too immature to be subjected to the harsh realities of war. For the same reasons that young people are protected from consuming alcohol at too young an age, they should also be protected from the danger of being killed in battle. As editor Murray Polner puts it, "All a draft can do is help transform yet another generation of Americans—*that's you*—into potential cannon fodder."

Paragraph 3

Secondly, America's students are the future of our country. Sending them to slaughter for political battles they are barely old enough to understand can only be viewed as a squandering of the nation's greatest resources. The military often lures young people in by offering them a chance to educate themselves and to learn computer, engineering, heavy industrial equipment, and other high-tech skills that can be applied in the private sector. As one senior Defense Department official explained, "We come to [recruits] and say, 'Well, which of these … training opportunities would entice you to join and stay with us?'" While it is great that the military offers soldiers these opportunities, it is unfair to tie them to war and death.

Paragraph 4

Finally, drafting students would only bring more violence into the lives of American youth. Young people are growing up in an increasingly violent culture, one that glorifies destruction and idolizes militarism, as evidenced by the

This is the essay's thesis statement. It lets the reader know upfront that this essay will argue that students should not be drafted.

This is the topic sentence of paragraph 2. Topic sentences do not always have to be the first sentence in the paragraph, but they should always state the paragraph's main point.

What is the topic sentence of paragraph 3?

Phrases like this one let you know the author is stating an opinion. Where else in this essay are opinions stated?

This is the topic sentence of paragraph 4. Note that it is a different topic than is covered in the other paragraphs.

popularity of violent video games, camouflage clothing, and Hummers. Reserve Officer Training Corps (ROTC) wings have penetrated our nation's campuses, even down to the High School level (with Junior ROTC becoming a feature in many high schools). Military recruiters sell the idea of service to students much the way that drug dealers string along dope addicts. Such recruiters are aggressive and often go against parents' wills in isolating students and pressuring them to sign up. The military already encroaches on our students' lives enough; a draft on students cannot be accepted.

Paragraph 5

There are many reasons why the draft should be opposed, but especially in defense of the nation's young people. War is typically conceived by politicians hidden away in grand office buildings and headquarters, and carried out by young people who at times are confused about whom they are fighting, and why. One author suggests, "If we want a society that is equal, cohesive, fair and war-resistant, let's fight for that, not punish our children for what we have allowed America to become." (Pollitt 9) It is immoral to make students bear the burden of decisions made by their elders in wartime.

Strong, opinionated quotes help accentuate your points and bring expert opinions into your essay.

Works Cited

Background Briefing on the All Volunteer Force, January 13, 2003. http://www.defenselink.mil/transcripts/transcript.aspx?transcriptid = 1252.

Polner, Murray. "A Military Draft After the Elections?" Veterans for Common Sense 24 Sept. 2004. < www.veteransforcommonsense.org/index.cfm?Page = Article&ID = 2066 > Accessed 23 May 2007.

Pollitt, Katha. "Do You Feel a Draft?" *Nation* 7 Jun 2004: 9.

Exercise 1A: Create an Outline from an Existing Essay

It often helps to create an outline of the five-paragraph essay before you write it. The outline can help you organize the information, arguments, and evidence you have gathered during your research.

For this exercise, create an outline that could have been used to write *Students Should Never Be Drafted Into the Military*. Identify topic sentences and provide at least two supporting details for each sentence. This "reverse engineering" exercise is meant to help familiarize you with how outlines can help classify and arrange information.

To do this you will need to

1. articulate the essay's thesis.
2. pinpoint important pieces of evidence.
3. flag quotes that supported the essay's ideas, and
4. identify key points that supported the argument.

Part of the outline has already been started to give you an idea of the assignment.

Outline

I. Paragraph One

Write the essay's thesis:

II. Paragraph Two

Topic: Students are young, impressionable, and too immature to be subjected to the harsh realities of war.

A. Young people need to be protected, the same way they need to be protected from the dangers of drinking alcohol too young.

B. Supporting evidence is Polner's quote about how young people end up as cannon fodder when they serve in the military.

III. Paragraph Three

Topic:

A.

B. Argument that opportunities to learn new skills should not be tied to military service.

IV. Paragraph Four

Topic:

A. Young people already live in a violent culture that glorifies destruction.

B.

V. Paragraph Five

A. Write the essay's conclusion:

Exercise 1B: Using Quotations to Enliven Your Essay

Quotations are an important part of every essay, and especially persuasive ones. Get in the habit of using quotes to support at least some of the ideas in your essays. Quotes do not need to appear in every paragraph, but often enough so that the essay contains voices aside from your own. When you write, use quotations to accomplish the following:

- Provide expert advice that you are not necessarily in the position to know about.
- Cite lively or passionate passages.
- Include a particularly well-written point that gets to the heart of the matter.
- Supply statistics or facts that have been derived from someone's research.
- Deliver anecdotes that illustrate the point you are trying to make.
- Express first-person testimony.

Problem One: Reread the essays presented in all sections of this book and find at least one example of each of the above quotation types.

There are a couple of important things to remember when using quotations.

- Note your sources' qualifications and biases. This way your reader can identify the person you have quoted and can put their words in a context.
- Put any quoted material within proper quotation marks. Failing to attribute quotes to their authors constitutes plagiarism, which is when an author takes someone else's words or ideas and presents them as their own. Plagiarism is a form of intellectual theft and must be avoided at all costs.

Students Should Be Drafted Into the Military

Editor's Notes The second model essay argues that students should be drafted into the military. The author explains why she believes that requiring young people to serve in the military benefits both them and society. The essay is structured as a five-paragraph essay in which each paragraph contributes a supporting piece of evidence to develop the argument.

As you read this essay, take note of its components and how they are organized (the sidebars in the margins provide further explanation).

▪ Refers to thesis and topic sentences

▫ Refers to supporting details

Paragraph 1

Protests on college campuses. Students burning draft cards. These and other events were part and parcel of the opposition to the Vietnam War, which was responsible for the dissolution in 1973 of mandatory military service in the United States. Since then, the U.S. army has been strictly voluntary and, while some students serve through ROTC and other programs, many American students do not have any ties to the military. However, careful consideration of both the problems and needs of our youngest citizens reveals that requiring young people to serve in the military after high school just might be the best thing for them.

What techniques does the author use when introducing the essay? Did it draw you in?

Paragraph 2

Requiring students to serve at least two years in the military could cure many of society's social ills that teens are directly involved in. Indeed, teens are responsible for much of our crime problems—according to the Office of Justice Programs,

What is the essay's thesis statement? How did you recognize it?

Statistics are used to bolster the author's point.

69

juveniles were involved in 12% of all violent crimes in 2003: 5% of murders, 12% of forcible rapes, 14% of robberies, and 12% of aggravated assaults. But military service could whip many of these young troublemakers into shape, disciplining and giving them a sense of right from wrong at the same time. As one writer argues, "Each passing generation produces teenagers who are more and more brazen, disrespectful, lazy and ill-qualified for success in the real world. Thus our society becomes more dangerous, depleted and dishonest every year." (Armstrong A11) But with mandatory military service, the government has a chance to lower the crime rate by putting the nation's youth through a rigorous and valuable behavioral program that will reduce their ability to cause crime. Some have even suggested that such a rigorous program would cut down on other ills that plague young people, such as obesity, smoking, and drug abuse.

In what way does the quote help support the paragraph's main idea? Also, note that it was taken from Viewpoint 5. Learn how to retain quotes that may be able to be used in your papers.

Paragraph 3

In addition, serving in the military is likely to benefit students by broadening their career options. Indeed, military service comes with a host of benefits, including reduced or paid-for tuition and training in high-tech and computer environments. Many who serve in the military go on to earn higher degrees and find they are very employable in a wide variety of industries. A former aviation electrician named Kathy O'Hara who served for 10 years in the Navy testified as much. "My time in the military," said O'Hara, "developed my ability to work as a team, communicate with those I work with, and how to work under stress. If that doesn't prepare a person for a career, I don't know what could." (qtd. in Friedman 1) If society truly wants to help its students, it seems obvious that requiring military service of students helps to prepare them for a more successful future.

What is the topic sentence of paragraph 3?

What qualifies O'Hara to speak on the issue of how the military can prepare a person for a career?

Paragraph 4

The ways in which a draft could help students is perhaps best evidenced by some of the nation's leading studies. These studies say high school students are not mature enough to

What words or phrases are used to keep the points in the essay moving?

immediately attend college, and recommend that students take a year or two off to work, travel, or otherwise grow up before they begin a serious program of study. Serving in the military could thus provide the perfect interim experience for high school students. History backs the wisdom of this; under the GI Bill, thousands of ex-soldiers returned to school in America, and succeeded in part because of the maturity they had gained in the field. This program was wildly successful, and many credit it with producing one of the most highly educated generations of Americans in the nation's history. Similarly, author Walt Shotwell envisions the draft to be "like extending high school for another two years," arguing "a two-year break after high school is valuable, even without a crisis." (11)

> This quote was taken from Viewpoint 1.

Paragraph 5

It seems clear that instituting a comprehensive national service program could help young people avoid the pitfalls of crime and substance abuse, while preparing them for a bright and successful future. If America truly wants to help its students reach their potential, requiring them to serve their country in military and social endeavors is an excellent way to start.

> Note how the conclusion recaps the essay's main theme without restating it.

Works Cited

Armstrong, Williams. "The U.S. Needs Mandatory Military Service." *Afro-American Red Star* Washington D.C. Vol. 114. Iss. 45 24–30 Jun. 2006: A11.

Shotwell, Walt. "We Need Universal Service Now." *Cityview* Vol. 14, Iss. 10, Des Moines, Iowa 9 Mar. 2006: 11.

Kathy O'Hara interviewed by Lauri S. Friedman, 24 May 2007.

Exercise 2A: Create an Outline from an Existing Essay

As you did for the first model essay in this section, create an outline that could have been used to write *Students Should Be Drafted*. Be sure to identify the essay's thesis statement, its supporting ideas, its descriptive passages, and key pieces of evidence that were used.

Exercise 2B: Identifying Persuasive Techniques

Essayists use many techniques to persuade you to agree with their ideas or to do something they want you to do. Some of the most common techniques are described in Preface B of this section, "The Persuasive Essay." These tools are facts and statistics, opinions, testimonials, examples and anecdotes, appeals to reason, appeals to emotion, ridicule and name-calling, and bandwagon. Go back to the preface and review these tools. Remember that most of these tools can be used to enhance your essay, but some of them—particularly ridiculing and name-calling—can detract from the essay's effectiveness. Nevertheless, you should be able to recognize them in the essays you read.

Some writers use one persuasive tool throughout their whole essay. For example, the essay may be one extended anecdote, or the writer may rely entirely on statistics. But most writers typically use a combination of persuasive tools. Model Essay 2, *Students Should Be Drafted*, does this.

Read Model Essay 2 again and see if you can find every persuasive tool used. Put that information in the following table. Part of the table is filled in for you. Explanatory notes are underneath the table. (NOTE: You will not fill in every box. No paragraph contains all of the techniques.)

	Paragraph 1 Sentence #	Paragraph 2 Sentence #	Paragraph 3 Sentence #	Paragraph 4 Sentence #	Paragraph 5 Sentence #
Fact					
Statistic					
Opinion				5[a]	
Testimonial			5–8[b]		
Example				6–9[c]	
Anecdote					
Appeal to Reason					
Appeal to Emotion			5–7[d]		
Ridicule					
Name-Calling					
Bandwagon					

NOTES

a. That serving in the military could be the perfect inter-im experience for high school students is an opinion; it is able to be argued with.

b. The author quotes a person who speaks from per-sonal experience.

c. The author uses the example of World War II and the GI Bill to show that the military can motivate students to pursue education once they have finished their service.

d. Imploring society to help students by drafting them is an appeal to emotion.

Now, look at the table you have produced. Which per-suasive tools does this essay rely on most heavily? Which are not used at all?

Apply this exercise to the other model essays in this sec-tion when you are finished reading them.

A Draft Will Hurt the Military

Editor's Notes The final model essay argues against the draft, arguing it would lower the quality of the military. This essay differs from the previous model essays because it is longer than five paragraphs. Sometimes five paragraphs are simply not enough to adequately develop an idea. Extending the length of an essay can allow the reader to explore a topic in more depth or present multiple pieces of evidence that together provide a complete picture of a topic. Longer essays can also help readers discover the complexity of a subject by examining a topic beyond its superficial exterior. Moreover, the ability to write a sustained research or position paper is a valuable skill you will need as you advance academically.

As you read, consider the questions posed in the margins. Continue to identify thesis statements, supporting details, transitions, and quotations. Examine the introductory and concluding paragraphs to understand how they give shape to the essay. Finally, evaluate the essay's general structure and assess its overall effectiveness.

■ Refers to thesis and topic sentences

■ Refers to supporting details

Paragraph 1

When people suggest reinstating the draft, they do so from the perspective that the more help the army has, the better it can carry out its missions. But what many people do not realize is that a draft would flood the military with unqualified, unspecialized people who do not really want to be there, which will make it an infinitely less effective fighting force. Maintaining the all-volunteer military is therefore the best way to ensure America has a dependable, motivated, and highly-skilled army for years to come.

What is the essay's thesis statement?

This information was presented in Viewpoint 2. Notice how the author has taken care to paraphrase the main ideas without copying the original wording.

What was the main idea of paragraph 2?

What is the topic sentence of paragraph 3?

What persuasive techniques are used in this essay?

Paragraph 2

For one, a draft would overwhelm the military. It would not have the resources, funds, or ability to care for and coordinate the flood of people that would be drafted. If all eligible men and women were really to be drafted, there would be millions of them. According to military historian Winston Groom, there are currently about 50 million Americans between ages 18 and 28, the typical age at which citizens would be drafted. Furthermore, 5 million additional people reach these ages every year. The military now operates with about 1 million soldiers—how would it possibly operate with all of those people filtering in and out of it? It would be inconceivable for the military to clothe, house, feed, and transport them, let alone adequately train and supply them. A draft would lower the quality of the military by burdening it with the care of millions of unnecessary people. (And if not all of them were drafted, it wouldn't be a true and equitable draft).

Paragraph 3

Secondly, reinstating the draft would lower the quality of the military by flooding it with people who are not really necessary to missions. The wars of the twenty-first century do not require huge reserves of soldiers, like wars of the past. World War I, World War II, and even the Vietnam War were fought soldier-to-soldier, in trenches, in scores of unfamiliar lands, cities, and villages. But hand-to-hand combat is rarely seen in modern warfare. The War on Terror and related battles rely more on high level intelligence work or operation of high tech equipment. What the military needs are skilled people to handle these tasks, rather than multitudes.

Paragraph 4

If people were drafted, they would likely serve for two years (as in the last drafted war, the Vietnam War). But two years is not enough to make a good soldier. Technology has so complicated a soldier's job that the military benefits most from specialists who have been trained over multiple tours of duty. "The insides of a Vietnam-era tank looked pretty much like an enclosed bulldozer. Today, the insides of our main battle tank look like the control room of the Starship Enterprise, and it takes years of specialized training to work the thing properly." (Groom) Nobody would argue that using soldiers who are committed to their branches of service for longer periods of time—even willing to make their careers there—is the best way to staff a modern military. Writes one former Marine officer, "Modern warfare requires that even the most junior infantryman master a wide array of technical and tactical skills. Honing these skills to reflex, a prerequisite for survival in combat, takes time…. One- or two-year terms, the longest that would be likely under conscription, would simply not allow for this comprehensive training." (Fick A19). And, just when drafted soldiers had finally learned how to do portions of their job, their rotation would end and the training would need to begin all over again with a new person.

What authors are quoted in this essay, and what are their qualifications?

Paragraph 5

Indeed, the American military is one of the most effective in the world precisely because of its high level of specialization. Of nations with the draft, just a handful have effective, first-class modern sleek fighting forces. One of these is Israel, whose citizens are drafted at 18 years old. But Israel is a tiny country with enormous, ongoing defense needs that would go disastrously unmet without the labor of all its citizens. Most of the other countries that draft citizens into their armies—Algeria, Bolivia, Cambodia, Ecuador, Estonia, Guatemala, Somalia, Thailand, and dozens of others—have a lot of bodies but are not world-renown for their sleek, effective fighting forces. As Groom has argued, "If you begin drafting people into the armed forces again, you can probably train them to shoot a rifle, salute, march and drill, load

What is the topic sentence of paragraph 5? What pieces of evidence are used to support it?

Make a list of all transitional words and phrases used in this essay.

an artillery piece, or swab the deck of a ship, just like in the old days. But the old days are gone. You won't get the dedication and special ability of the professionals we already have. What you will get instead is a gigantic, useless mob of half-trained malcontents whose skills are half-a-century outdated. The world already has too many militaries like that."

Paragraph 6

What is the topic sentence of paragraph 6?

Finally, the U.S. military will never have soldiers as good as those who truly want to be there. One former soldier who served in the Vietnam War remembers the apathy, resentment, and lack of commitment that drafted soldiers had towards their mission. "Quite a few of them didn't want to be there, and their attitudes showed it... Their hearts just weren't in it—and who could blame them? They would likely have fought hard and well in a 'popular war' such as World War II, but Vietnam wasn't popular, and most felt they had been victims of the bad luck of the draw." (Groom) Using drafted soldiers is the worst way to approach modern conflicts because they, unlike wars of the past, have no clearly defined beginning and end; to persevere, soldiers will need to recall the reasons why they signed up for service in the first place.

Paragraph 7

Note how the conclusion helps bookend the ideas presented in the essay.

All of these reasons are why one former Marine officer has called the reinstatement of the draft "a dumbing down of the institution." (Fick) If the current all-volunteer military is stretched too thin to adequately perform, it is not because it is short on soldiers. Instead, it is because the American government has been reluctant to spend appropriate monies that could expand the force, offering new equipment and more time off for soldiers. Writes one soldier who saw action in Iraq: "For now, expanding the volunteer force would give us a larger military without the inherent liabilities of conscription." (Fick A19) We should respect our soldiers by giving them the equipment they need, not by flooding their ranks with unspecialized people who don't want to be there.

Works Cited

Fick, Nathaniel. "Don't Dumb Down the Military." *New York Times* 20 Jul. 2004: A19.

Groom, Winston. "An Army of 50 Million? The Surpassingly Dishonest Draft Debate." *Weekly Standard* 11 Dec. 2006.

Exercise 3A: Create an Outline for Your Own Essay

The final model essay expresses a particular point of view about the military draft. For this exercise, your assignment is to find supporting ideas, choose specific and concrete details, create an outline, and ultimately write a five-paragraph essay making a different, or even opposing, point about the military draft. Your goal is to use persuasive techniques to convince your reader.

Step I: Write a thesis statement.

The following thesis statement would be appropriate for an opposing essay on why instituting a draft would improve the quality of the military, and improve society:

> If every American served in some capacity, not only would our troops get the relief they desperately need, but thousands of others could participate in Peace-Corps-like social works projects that would benefit all Americans.

Or, see the sample paper topics suggested in Appendix D for more ideas.

Step II: Brainstorm pieces of supporting evidence.

Using information from some of the viewpoints in the previous section and from the information found in Section III of this book, write down three arguments or pieces of evidence that support the thesis statement you selected. Then, for each of these three arguments, write down supportive facts, examples, and details that support it. These could be:

- statistical information
- personal memories and anecdotes
- quotes from experts, peers, or family members
- observations of people's actions and behaviors
- specific and concrete details

Supporting pieces of evidence for the above sample thesis statement are found in this book, and include:

- Walt Shortwell's suggestion in Viewpoint 1 for a comprehensive national service program that would allow Americans to participate in either military, social, environmental, and infrastructure improvement programs.
- The fact that in the early 1940s more than 6.3 million recruits were inducted in the U.S. military, indicating that the army is capable of providing for millions of draftees.
- The claim made by Armstrong Williams in Viewpoint 5 that conscription would cut down on obesity, drug abuse, smoking, and crime.

Step III: Place the information from Step I in outline form.

Step IV: Write the arguments or supporting statements in paragraph form.

By now you have three arguments that support the essay's thesis statement, as well as supporting material. Use the outline to write out your three supporting arguments in paragraph form. Make sure each paragraph has a topic sentence that states the paragraph's thesis clearly and broadly. Then, add supporting sentences that express the facts, quotes, details, and examples that support the paragraph's argument. The paragraph may also have a concluding or summary sentence.

Every essay features introductory and concluding paragraphs that are used to frame the main ideas being presented. Along with presenting the essay's thesis statement, well-written introductions should grab the attention of the reader and make clear why the topic being explored is important. The conclusion reiterates the essay's thesis and is also the last chance for the writer to make an impression on the reader. Strong introductions and conclusions can greatly enhance an essay's effect on an audience.

The Introduction

There are several techniques that can be used to craft an introductory paragraph. An essay can start with:

- an anecdote: a brief story that illustrates a point relevant to the topic;
- startling information: facts or statistics that elucidate the point of the essay;
- setting up and knocking down a position: a position or claim believed by proponents of one side of a controversy, followed by statements that challenge that claim;
- historical perspective: an example of the way things used to be that leads into a discussion of how or why things work differently now;
- summary information: general introductory information about the topic that feeds into the essay's thesis statement.

Problem One

Reread the introductory paragraphs of the model essays and of the viewpoints in Section I. Identify which of the techniques described above are used in the example essays. How do they grab the attention of the reader? Are their thesis statements clearly presented?

Problem Two

Write an introduction for the essay you have outlined and partially written in Exercise 3A using one of the techniques described above.

The Conclusion

The conclusion brings the essay to a close by summarizing or returning to its main ideas. Good conclusions, however, go beyond simply repeating these ideas. Strong conclusions explore a topic's broader implications and reiterate why it is important to consider. They may frame the essay by returning to an anecdote featured in the opening paragraph. Or, they may close with a quotation or refer back to an event in the essay. In opinionated essays, the conclusion can reiterate which side the essay is taking or ask the reader to reconsider a previously held position on the subject.

Problem Three

Reread the concluding paragraphs of the model essays and of the viewpoints in Section I. Which were most effective in driving their arguments home to the reader? What sorts of techniques did they use to do this? Did they appeal emotionally to the reader, or bookend an idea or event referenced elsewhere in the essay?

Problem Four

Write a conclusion for the essay you have outlined and partially written in Exercise 3A using one of the techniques described above.

Write Your Own Expository Five-Paragraph Essay

Using the information from this book, write your own five-paragraph persuasive essay that deals with the military draft. You can use the resources in this book for information about issues relating to this topic and how to structure this type of essay.

The following steps are suggestions on how to get started.

Step One: Choose your topic.

The first step is to decide what topic to write your persuasive essay on. Is there any subject that particularly fascinates you? Is there an issue you strongly support, or feel strongly against? Is there a topic you feel personally connected to or one that you would like to learn more about? Ask yourself such questions before selecting your essay topic. Refer to Appendix D: Sample Essay Topics if you need help selecting a topic.

Step Two: Write down questions and answers about the topic.

Before you begin writing, you will need to think carefully about what ideas your essay will contain. This is a process known as *brainstorming*. Brainstorming involves asking yourself questions and coming up with ideas to discuss in your essay. Possible questions that will help you with the brainstorming process include:

- Why is this topic important?
- Why should people be interested in this topic?
- How can I make this essay interesting to the reader?
- What question am I going to address in this paragraph or essay?
- What facts, ideas, or quotes can I use to support the answer to my question?

Questions especially for persuasive essays include:

- Is there something I want to convince my reader of?
- Is there a topic I want to advocate in favor of, or rally against?
- Is there enough evidence to support my opinion?
- Do I want to make a call to action – motivate my readers to do something about a particular problem or event?

Step Three: Gather facts, ideas, and anecdotes related to your topic.

This book contains several places to find information, including the viewpoints and the appendices. In addition, you may want to research the books, articles, and Web sites listed in Section III, or do additional research in your local library. You can also conduct interviews if you know someone who has a compelling story that would fit well in your essay.

Step Four: Develop a workable thesis statement.

Use what you have written down in steps two and three to help you articulate the main point or argument you want to make in your essay. It should be expressed in a clear sentence and make an arguable or supportable point.

Example:

The military is too critical an institution to be staffed with people who do not really want to be there.

(This could be the thesis statement of a persuasive essay that argues that instituting a military draft would force unskilled, apathetic people to serve as soldiers, which would lower the quality of the American military.)

Step Five: Write an outline or diagram.

- a. Write the thesis statement at the top of the outline.
- b. Write roman numerals I, II, and III on the left side of the page.

c. Next to each roman numeral, write down the best ideas you came up with in step three. These should all directly relate to and support the thesis statement.

d. Next to each letter write down information that supports that particular idea.

Step Six: Write the three supporting paragraphs.
Use your outline to write the three supporting paragraphs. Write down the main idea of each paragraph in sentence form. Do the same thing for the supporting points of information. Each sentence should support the paragraph of the topic. Be sure you have relevant and interesting details, facts, and quotes. Use transitions when you move from idea to idea to keep the text fluid and smooth. Sometimes, although not always, paragraphs can include a concluding or summary sentence that restates the paragraph's argument.

Step Seven: Write the introduction and conclusion.
See Exercise 3B for information on writing introductions and conclusions.

Step Eight: Read and rewrite.
As you read, check your essay for the following:

- ✔ Does the essay maintain a consistent tone?
- ✔ Do all paragraphs reinforce your general thesis?
- ✔ Do all paragraphs flow from one to the other? Do you need to add transition words or phrases?
- ✔ Have you quoted from reliable, authoritative, and interesting sources?
- ✔ Is there a sense of progression throughout the essay?
- ✔ Does the essay get bogged down in too much detail or irrelevant material?
- ✔ Does your introduction grab the reader's attention?
- ✔ Does your conclusion reflect back on any previously discussed material, or give the essay a sense of closure?
- ✔ Are there any spelling or grammatical errors?

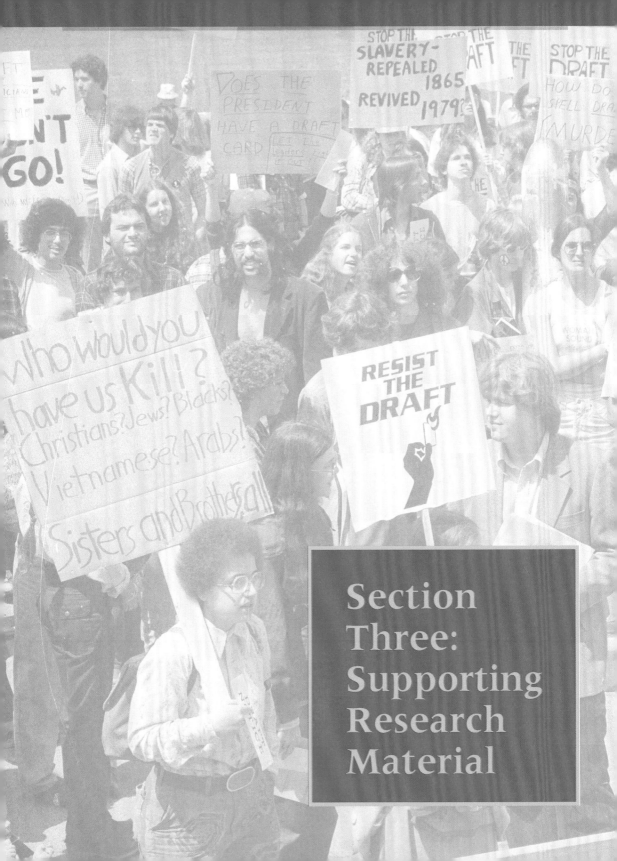

Section Three: Supporting Research Material

Facts About the Military and the Military Draft

American Opinions About a Military Draft

According to a 2005 AP-Ipsos poll, seven in 10 Americans say they oppose reinstatement of the draft, and almost half of those polled strongly oppose reinstatement. About a quarter of American say they favor reinstating the draft.

A CNN-USA *Today* poll conducted in June 2005 found that 85 percent of Americans surveyed opposed a return to a military draft.

A 2004 poll conducted by the Alliance for Security found that 52 percent of those eligible for the draft would either actively seek deferment or refuse to serve if the draft was to be reinstated.

According to a Gallup poll in the summer of 2005, 62 percent of Americans surveyed said they oppose compelling all 18-year-old men to receive a year of military training followed by mandatory reserve service.

Efficacy of a Draft

A 2004 study that compared the efficacy of draftees to volunteers found that volunteer soldiers tend to serve longer than draftees.

In the Air Force, volunteers (figures based on 1969 pre-all volunteer force numbers) served 20 percent longer than draftees.

In the Marine Corps, volunteers served 19 percent longer than draftees.

In the Navy, volunteers served 18 percent longer than draftees.

In the Army, volunteers served 43 percent longer than draftees.

Who Serves in the Military Today?

- According to the U.S. Department of Defense, as of October 2005 the United States had some 2.6 million active and reserve service members in the armed forces.
- As of September 2005, the Selective Service System had 13.5 million names of males age eighteen to twenty-five on its registration rolls.
- As of fall 2005, nearly 96 percent of all men aged 18 to 26 had complied with draft registration, according to the Selective Service System.
- According to the U.S. Department of Labor, 85 percent of the current personnel of the Armed Forces are enlisted, while 15 percent are officers.
- According to the U.S. Department of Defense, the breakdown of military personnel by race in 2002 for enlisted men was 64 percent white, 20 percent black, 10 percent Latino, and 6 percent Asian and other. For officers, the breakdown was 83 percent white, 9 percent black, 4 percent Latino, and 5 percent Asian and other.
- According to the Bureau of Labor Statistics, the average age of enlisted military accessions is 20.1 years.
- In 2005 the Army repeatedly missed its monthly recruiting goals, falling short by 42 percent in April 2005.

Historical Use of the Draft in America

- The U.S. Constitution does not specifically authorize a draft, but it does authorize Congress to "raise and support Armies."
- The Confederacy began drafting men in April 1862, nearly a year before the Union instituted a draft. (Source: U.S. Constitution Online)
- The Selective Service Act was passed by Congress during World War I; it established the Selective Service System and conscripted men aged 21–30.

- According to the Selective Service System, the first peacetime draft in the U.S. was enacted in 1940, a year before the Japanese attacked Pearl Harbor.
- According to the Selective Service System, 3.3 million were drafted in 1943—the most ever in one year—during the peak of World War II.
- 2.8 million soldiers were drafted into the Army during World War I.
- 10.1 million soldiers were drafted into the army during World War II.
- 1.5 million soldiers were drafted to fight in the Korean War.
- 1.9 million soldiers were drafted into the Vietnam War.
- The smallest number of draftees (646) was in 1973.
- During the Korean Conflict (1950-53), World War II veterans were exempt from the draft.
- In January 2003 New York Congressman Charles Rangel introduced a bill to bring back the draft, but it was unpopular and swiftly voted down.
- The U.S. army discontinued the draft in 1973, moving to an all-volunteer system that it continues to maintain.

The Draft Around the World

The following countries have a strict draft that requires a segment of the population to serve in the military with little exception:

Afghanistan; Albania; Algeria; Angola; Bolivia; Cambodia; Chile; China; Colombia; Cuba; Dominican Republic; Ecuador; Egypt; El Salvador; Equatorial Guinea; Estonia; Ethiopia; Georgia; Greece; Guatemala; Guinea; Guinea-Bissau; Honduras; Iran; Iraq; Israel; Kazakhstan; Laos; Lebanon; Liberia; Libya; Madagascar; Mexico; Mongolia; Morocco; Mozambique; North

Korea; Paraguay; Peru; Philippines; Romania; Singapore; Somalia; South Korea; Sudan; Thailand; Tunisia; Turkey; Venezuela; Vietnam; Yemen.

The following countries have no draft:

Antigua and Barbuda; Australia; Bahamas; Bahrain; Bangladesh; Barbados; Belgium; Belize; Botswana; Brunei Darussalam; Burkina Faso; Burundi; Cameroon; Canada; Costa Rica; Djibouti; Fiji; Gabon; Gambia; Ghana; Grenada; Haiti; Hong Kong; Iceland; India; Ireland; Jamaica; Japan; Jordan: Kenya; Kyrgyzstan; Lesotho; Luxembourg; Malawi; Malaysia; Maldives; Malta; Mauritania; Mauritius; Monaco; Myanmar; Nepal; Netherlands; New Zealand; Nicaragua; Nigeria; Oman; Pakistan; Panama; Papua New Guinea; Qatar; Rwanda; San Marino; Saudi Arabia; Sierra Leone; South Africa; Sri Lanka; Suriname; Swaziland; Tonga; Trinidad and Tobago; Uganda; United Arab Emirates; United Kingdom of Great Britain and Northern Ireland; United States; Uruguay; Vanuatu; Zambia; Zimbabwe.

If the Draft Is Reinstated

According to the Selective Service System:

- In the event the draft was reinstated, college students could have their induction postponed until the end of the current semester. (This would allow for seniors to finish their academic year.)
- Married men, or men with a dependent child, would not receive any special treatment. (In the past, a married man who was also a father could receive a "hardship to dependents" deferment.)
- A lottery based on birthdays determines the order in which registered men are called up for duty. The first to be called, in a sequence determined by the lottery, will be men whose twentieth birthday falls during that

year, followed, if needed, by 21–25-year-olds and then by 18- and 19-year-olds.

Women and the Military

- In 1948, President Harry S. Truman signed the Women's Armed Services Integration Act, which allowed women into the regular Army and the Organized Reserve Corps.
- More than 2,000 women volunteered as nurses (many serving on the battlefield) during the Civil War. One of the key figures in the volunteer effort was Clara Barton, who founded the American Red Cross in 1881.
- According to the Selective Service System, more than 150,000 women volunteered to serve during World War II. The Women's Army Auxiliary Corps (WAAC) was formed in 1941 to allow women to serve in clerical and support roles in the Army.
- The Defense Manpower Data Center (DMDC) reports that as of 2004, 20.2 percent of all active applicants for military service were women.
- According to the U.S. Census Bureau, women make up 16 percent of veterans of the Persian Gulf War (1990-91). In contrast, fewer than 5 percent of veterans from earlier wars were women.
- Women have never been drafted, even during war time; in order to do so, Congress would have to amend the Selective Service law to add women to the draft.

What About Those Who Are Opposed to War?

- Those opposed to war but obliged to serve are called "conscientious objectors."
- The first claim for conscientious objector status in America was in 1658; "conscientious objector" was officially recognized as a noncombatant category during the Civil War.

- According to Mothers Against the Draft, during the Civil War both Northern and Southern men who did not want to fight could hire "substitutes" to take their place in the draft for $300.
- The Selective Service offers alternative service programs for those who are classified as conscientious objectors to military action for religious or moral reasons, but all males must register regardless of their beliefs.
- According to the Canadian Broadcasting Corporation, as many as 125,000 draft-age men fled to Canada to avoid being drafted by the United States during the Vietnam War.
- According to federal law, failing to register with the Selective Service can result in penalties of as much as $250,000, a prison term of up to five years, or both if tried and convicted.
- Mothers Against the Draft reports that the anti-war protests and riots of the 1960s against the Vietnam War were the first such riots in the United States since the Civil War.

Finding and Using Sources of Information

No matter what type of essay you are writing, it is necessary to find information to support your point of view. You can use sources such as books, magazine articles, newspaper articles, and online articles.

Using Books and Articles

You can find books and articles in a library by using the library's computer or cataloging system. If you are not sure how to use these resources, ask a librarian to help you. You can also use a computer to find many magazine articles and other articles written specifically for the Internet.

You are likely to find a lot more information than you can possibly use in your essay, so your first task is to narrow it down to what is likely to be most usable. Look at book and article titles. Look at book chapter titles, and examine the book's index to see if it contains information on the specific topic you want to write about. (For example, if you want to write about the draft and you find a book about the Vietnam War, check the chapter titles and index to be sure it contains information relating to the military draft before you bother to check out the book.)

For a five–paragraph essay, you do not need a great deal of supporting information, so quickly try to narrow down your materials to a few good books and magazine or Internet articles. You do not need dozens. You might even find that one or two good books or articles contain all the information you need.

You probably do not have time to read an entire book, so find the chapters or sections that relate to your topic, and skim these. When you find useful information, copy it onto a note card or notebook. You should look for supporting facts, statistics, quotations, and examples.

Using the Internet

When you select your supporting information, it is important that you evaluate its source. This is especially important with information you find on the Internet. Because nearly anyone can put information on the Internet, there is as much bad information as good information. Before using Internet information—or any information—try to determine if the source seems to be reliable. Is the author or Internet site sponsored by a legitimate organization? Is it from a government source? Does the author have any special knowledge or training relating to the topic you are looking up? Does the article give any indication of where its information comes from?

Using Your Supporting Information

When you use supporting information from a book, article, interview or other source, there are three important things to remember:

1. *Make it clear whether you are using a direct quotation or a paraphrase.* If you copy information directly from your source, you are quoting it. You must put quotation marks around the information, and tell where the information comes from. If you put the information in your own words, you are paraphrasing it.

Here is an example of a using a quotation:

> Increasingly, the military is made up of poor and disadvantaged citizens, and rarely the nation's most privileged. Author William Broyles, Jr. believes that instituting a draft would correct these inequities by forcing the nation's wealthy citizens to serve as well. "If this war is truly worth fighting, then the burdens of doing so should fall on all Americans," he argues.

Here is an example of a brief paraphrase of the same passage:

> Increasingly, the military is made up of poor and disadvantaged citizens, and rarely the nation's most privileged. Author William Broyles, Jr. believes that instituting a draft would correct these inequities by forcing the nation's wealthy citizens to serve as well. It is unfair that wars should be fought only by one sector of society; if the war is just, then all Americans should join together to stand up for their country.

2. *Use the information fairly.* Be careful to use supporting information in the way the author intended it. For example, it is unfair to quote an author as saying, "Reinstating the draft could be a good way of inciting nationalism and political activism in our nation's youth" when he or she intended to say, "Reinstating the draft could be a good way of inciting nationalism and political activism in our nation's youth, but it seems a most dangerous and ineffective way to get young Americans interested in their country's affairs." This is called taking information out of context. This is using supporting evidence unfairly.

3. *Give credit where credit is due.* Giving credit is known as citing. You must use citations when you use someone else's information, but not every piece of supporting information needs a citation.

   - If the supporting information is general knowledge—that is, it can be found in many sources—you do not have to cite your source.
   - If you directly quote a source, you must cite it.
   - If you paraphrase information from a specific source, you must cite it.

If you do not use citations where you should, you are *plagiarizing*—or stealing—someone else's work.

Citing Your Sources

There are a number of ways to cite your sources. Your teacher will probably want you to do it in one of three ways:

- Informal: As in the example in number 1 above, tell where you got the information as you present it in the text of your essay.
- Informal list: At the end of your essay, place an unnumbered list of all the sources you used. This tells the reader where, in general, your information came from.
- Formal: Use numbered footnotes. Footnotes are generally placed at the end of an article or essay, although they may be placed elsewhere depending on your teacher's requirements.

Works Cited

Broyles, Jr., William. "A War for Us, Fought by Them." *New York Times* 4 Mar. 2004: A29.

Using MLA Style to Create a Works Cited List

You will probably need to create a list of works cited for your paper. These include materials that you quoted from, relied heavily on, or consulted to write your paper. There are several different ways to structure these references. The following examples are based on Modern Language Association (MLA) style, one of the major citation styles used by writers.

Book Entries

For most book entries you will need the author's name, the book's title, where it was published, what company published it, and the year it was published. This information is usually found on the inside of the book. Variations on book entries include the following:

A Book by a Single Author
Guest, Emma. *Children of AIDS: Africa's Orphan Crisis.* London: Sterling, 2003.

Two or More Books by the Same Author
Friedman, Thomas L. *The World Is Flat: A Brief History of the Twentieth Century.* New York: Farrar, Straus and Giroux, 2005.

---. *From Beirut to Jerusalem.* New York: Doubleday, 1989.

A Book by Two or More Authors
Pojman, Louis P., and Jeffrey Reiman. *The Death Penalty: For and Against.* Lanham, MD: Rowman & Littlefield, 1998.

A Book with an Editor
> Friedman, Lauri S., ed. *At Issue: What Motivates Suicide Bombers?* San Diego, CA: Greenhaven, 2004.

Periodical and Newspaper Entries

Entries for sources found in periodicals and newspapers are cited a bit differently than books. For one, these sources usually have a title and a publication name. They also may have specific dates and page numbers. Unlike book entries, you do not need to list where newspapers or periodicals are published or what company publishes them.

An Article from a Periodical
> Snow, Keith Harmon. "State Terror in Ethiopia." *Z Magazine* Jun. 2004: 33–35.

An Unsigned Article from a Periodical
> "Broadcast Decency Rules." *Issues & Controversies on File* 30 Apr. 2004.

An Article from a Newspaper
> Constantino, Rebecca. "Fostering Love, Respecting Race." *Los Angeles Times* 14 Dec. 2002: B17.

Internet Sources

To document a source you found online, try to provide as much information on it as possible, including the author's name, the title of the document, date of publication or of last revision, the URL, and your date of access.

A Web Source

Shyovitz, David. "The History and Development of Yiddish." Jewish Virtual Library. 30 May 2005 < http://www.jewishvirtuallibrary.org/jsource/History/yiddish.html. > . Accessed September 11, 2007.

Your teacher will tell you exactly how information should be cited in your essay. Generally, the very least information needed is the original author's name and the name of the article or other publication.

Be sure you know exactly what information your teacher requires before you start looking for your supporting information so that you know what information to include with your notes.

Sample Essay Topics

The U.S. Needs a Draft

The U.S. Does Not Need a Draft

A Draft Can Help the U.S. Meet Current Military Needs

A Draft Is Not Useful for Twenty-First Century Conflict

A Draft Will Invigorate the Military

A Draft Will Weaken the Military

A Draft Will Improve Soldiers' Experience in the Military

A Draft Will Downgrade the Quality of the Military

The Draft Should Require People to Serve in either Military or Civilian Roles

A Draft Will Unify the Nation

A Draft Will Incite Political Riots around the Nation

A Draft Will Militarize Society

A Draft Will Make Americans More Patriotic

A Draft Will Make Young Americans More Likely to Oppose War

A Draft Will Not Make Young Americans More Likely to Oppose War

A Draft Will Make Society More Charitable

Students Should Be Drafted

Students Should Not Be Drafted

Women Should Be Drafted

Women Should Not Be Drafted

A Draft Will Make the Military Service More Equal

Military Service is Already Equal

Minorities and the Poor Disproportionately Serve in the Military

The Military Is Well-Rounded

The Children of Politicians Should Serve in Wars

The Children of Politicians Will Likely be Able to Avoid a Draft

Instituting a Draft Violates the Rights of Americans Who Oppose War

Organizations to Contact

American Civil Liberties Union
125 Broad Street, 18th Floor, New York, NY 10004-2400
• (800) 567-ACLU • Web site: www.aclu.org

The American Civil Liberties Union works to defend to rights and freedoms of individuals on a variety of issues, including the draft. The ACLU comes to the aid, for example, of those seeking conscientious objector status but who are nonetheless called to serve in battle.

Center for Military Readiness
P. O. Box 51600, Livonia, MI 48151 • (202) 347-5333 •
e-mail: info@cmrlink.org • Web site: www.cmrlink.org

The Center for Military Readiness is an educational organization that focuses on issues concerning military personnel. It promotes high standards in military training and efficiency. It believes the most important issue for the military is to deter aggression whenever possible and to protect the United States.

Center on Conscience and War (CCW)
1830 Connecticut Avenue NW, Washington, DC 20009 • (202) 483-2220 • (800) 379-2679 • e-mail: ccw@centeronconscience.org • Web site: www. centeronconscience.org

The Center of Conscience and War is an association of religious bodies that work together to defend the rights of conscientious objectors. It is opposed to all types of military conscription.

Eagle Forum

P.O. Box 618, Alton, IL 62002 • (618) 462-5415 • e-mail: eagle@eagleforum.org • Web site: www.eagleforum.org

Founded by Phyllis Schlafly, best known as a champion against the proposed Equal Rights Amendment, the Eagle Forum provides a "pro-family" perspective on a variety of issues including the military draft, in particular the question of whether women should be drafted or allowed to serve in combat with men.

Friends Committee on National Legislation (FCNL)

245 Second Street NE, Washington, DC 20002 • (202) 547-6000 • (800) 630-1330 • Web site: www.fcnl.org

Founded during World War II by the Religious Society of Friends (Quakers), FCNL is the largest peace lobby in Washington DC. It played an instrumental role in the development of the Peace Corps in the early 1960s. In addition to a number of pamphlets and brochures, FCNL also publishes a monthly newsletter.

Mothers Against the Draft

P.O. Box 656, Sparks, NV 89432 • (775) 356-9009 • e-mail: info@mothersagainstthedraft.org • Web site: www.mothersagainstthedraft.org

Mothers Against the Draft was founded by a group of concerned mothers from across the political spectrum who oppose the reinstatement of compulsory military service. They believe that the U.S. military is dangerously overextended and they oppose pre-emptive military actions that will of necessity increase the number of troops needed in combat. They also oppose drafting women and placing current women soldiers in combat.

Project for Youth and Non-Military Opportunities (Project YANO)

P.O. Box 230157, Encinitas, CA 92023 • (760) 634-3604 • e-mail: projyano@aol.com • Web site: www. projectyano.org

Project YANO focuses on low-income and minority students and provides them with information about the military as well as alternatives to military enlistment. The founders of Project YANO believe that low-income and minority youths are disproportionately targeted for military recruitment, often with false expectations about what to expect from military service.

Selective Service System

National Headquarters, Arlington, VA 22209-2405 • (703) 605-4100 • e-mail: information@sss.gov • Web site: www.sss.gov

The Selective Service System, an independent federal agency, oversees conscription of eligible individuals to serve in the military in the event of a need for extra manpower (such as a declaration of war). It is also charged with finding alternative service programs for anyone classified as a conscientious objector. In addition to numerous surveys and reports for the U.S. Government, the Selective Service also publishes a bimonthly newsletter, *The Register*.

U.S. Department of Defense

The Pentagon, Washington, DC 20301 • Web site: www. dod.gov

Encompassing the Army, Navy, Air Force, Marines, Coast Guard, and National Guard, the Department of Defense is the agency responsible for providing military forces and equipment to protect the United States from attack. It was created in 1949 by an act of Congress and is headquartered in the Pentagon, one of the most recognizable office complexes in the world. The Department of Defense oversees more than three million active duty and reserve troops.

U.S. Department of Homeland Security (DHS)

Washington, DC 20528 • (202) 282-8010 • Web site: www.dhs.gov

Created in response to the terrorist attacks on New York and Washington on September 11, 2001, The Department of Homeland Security united functions of the Departments of Justice, Treasure, Defense, Energy, Commerce, Agriculture, and Transportation under one umbrella. The goal of DHS is to streamline the operations of these diverse offices as a means of further protecting the United States from enemy attacks.

U.S. Department of Veterans Affairs

810 Vermont Avenue NW, Washington, DC 20420 • (800) 827-1000 • Web site: www.va.gov

The Department of Veterans Affairs, a Cabinet-level agency since 1989, oversees such veterans' issues as pensions, long-term care, and insurance, burial, and survivor benefits. With origins dating back to 1636, the Veterans Affairs department serves 25 million living veterans and another 45 million spouses and dependents of veterans.

Veterans of Foreign Wars (VFW)

200 Maryland Ave NE, Washington, DC 20002 • (202)543-2239 • e-mail vfw@vfwdc.org • Web site: www.wfw.org

With some 2.4 million members and 9,000 posts around the world, VFW looks after the needs of those who served in the U.S. armed forces. It has worked to improve benefits for veterans, such as medical care and fair compensation. VFW also works to educate the public about the role the military plays in society and the importance of contributing to society by providing some sort of service.

Bibliography

Books

Martin Anderson, ed. (with Barbara Honegger), *The Military Draft: Selected Readings on Conscription*. Stanford, CA: Hoover Institute Press, 1982.

John Whiteclay Chambers, *To Raise an Army*. New York: Free Press, 1987.

Eliot A. Cohen, *Citizens and Soldiers: The Dilemmas of Military Service*. Ithaca, NY: Cornell University Press, 1990.

Jerry Elmer, *Felon for Peace: The Memoir of a Vietnam-Era Draft Resister*. Nashville, TN: Vanderbilt University Press, 2005.

Tod Ensign, ed. *America's Military Today: The Challenge of American Militarism*. New York: W.W. Norton, 2004.

Nathaniel C. Fick, *One Bullet Away: The Making of a Marine Officer*. New York: Houghton Mifflin, 2005.

George Q. Flynn, *Conscription and Democracy: The Draft in France, Great Britain, and the United States*. Westport, CT: Greenwood Press, 2001.

Philip Gold, *The Coming Draft: The Crisis in Our Military and Why Selective Service is Wrong for America*. New York: Presidio Press, 2006.

Robert K. Griffith, *United States Army's Transition to the All-Volunteer Force, 1968–74*. Washington, DC: Department of the Army, 1997.

R. Charles Johnson and Charles E. Sherman, *Draft Registration and the Law: A Guidebook*. Occidental, CA: Nolo Press, 1991.

Stephen M. Kohn, *Jailed for Peace: The History of American Draft Law Violators, 1658–1985*. Westport, CT: Greenwood Press, 1986.

Frank Kusch, *All American Boys: Draft Dodgers in Canada from the Vietnam War.* Westport, CT: Praeger Publishers, 2001.

Michael S. Neiberg, *Making Citizen-Soldiers: ROTC and the Ideology of American Military Service.* Cambridge, MA: Harvard University Press, 2001.

Michael E. O'Hanlon, *Defense Strategy for the Post-Saddam Era.* Washington, DC: Brookings Institution Press, 2005.

Kathy Roth-Douquet and Frank Schaeffer, *AWOL: The Unexcused Absence of America's Upper Classes from the Military—And How It Hurts Our Country.* New York: Collins, 2006.

David R. Segal, *Recruiting for Uncle Sam: Citizenship and Military Manpower.* Lawrence, KS: University Press of Kansas, 1992.

James Tracy, ed. *The Military Draft Handbook: A Brief History and Practical Advice for the Curious and Concerned.* San Francisco, Manic D Press, 2005.

Periodicals

Phillip Carter and Paul Glastris, "The Case for the Draft," *Washington Monthly,* March 2005, pp. 18–25.

Elaine Donnelly, "Will Women Be Forced into Selective Service?" *Human Events,* August 15, 2005.

Thomas Donnelly, "Force Size and Strategy," *National Security Outlook,* September 2004.

Tod Ensign, "Draft Chatter," *Toward Freedom,* Fall 2004.

Nathaniel Fick, "Don't Dumb Down the Military," *New York Times,* July 20, 2004, p. A19.

Herb Field, "Bring Back the Draft—But Don't Look for Bush White House to Take Action," *The Patriot News,* Harrisburg, PA, May 18, 2005.

Joseph Gainza, "Will There Be a Draft?" *Peacework,* November 2004.

Juan Gonzales, "Racial Divide Evident in Military," *New York Daily News,* November 8, 2005.

William Norman Grigg, "Get Ready for the Draft," *The New American,* May 30, 2005.

Bob Herbert, "War on the Cheap," *Liberal Opinion Week,* December 27, 2004.

Tom Infield, "Peace-Churches Plan Alternatives to Military Draft," *Philadelphia Inquirer,* June 19, 2005.

Frederick W. Kagan, "The War Against Reserves," *National Security Outlook,* August 2005.

Fred Kaplan, "Who's In the Army Now?" *Slate,* June 30, 2005.

Tim Kane, "Who Are the Recruits?" Heritage Foundation, October 26, 2006. www.heritage.org/Research/NationalSecurity/cda05-08.cfm.

Tim Kane, "No Justification for a Military Draft," *Human Events,* November 29, 2006.

William R. King, "Our Nation Needs Everyone," *Pittsburgh Post-Gazette,* June 12, 2006, p. J2.

Brad Knickerbocker, "Behind Talk of a New Draft," *Christian Science Monitor,* November 22, 2006.

Robert C. Koehler, "Counter-Recruiters: All the Charm of the Draft + ," *The Human Quest,* July–August 2005.

Lawrence J. Korb, "All-Volunteer Army Shows Signs of Wear," *Atlanta Journal-Constitution,* February 27, 2005.

John Lehman, "Diversity and the Draft," *Washington Post,* February 3, 2003.

Francis X. Maier, "Biting the Bullet," *Crisis,* January 2005.

Lori Manning, "Military Women: Who They Are, What They Do, and Why It Matters," *Women's Review of Books,* February 2004, pp. 7–9.

Charles Moskos, "A New Concept of the Citizen-Soldier," *Orbis,* Fall 2005.

Charles Moskos, "Feel that Draft?" *Chicago Tribune,* June 8, 2005, p. 23.

Michael E. O'Hanlon, "Forget About Military Draft," *Japan Times,* January 29, 2003.

Clarence Page, "Burning the Draft Card," *Liberal Opinion Week,* October 18, 2004.

Robert Pear, "U.S. Has Contingency Plans for Draft of Medical Workers," *New York Times,* October 19, 2004.

Murray Polner, "A Military Draft After the Elections?" Veterans for Common Sense, September 24, 2004.

Pamela M. Prah, "Draft Debates," *CQ Researcher,* August 19, 2005.

Anna Quindlen, "Leaving on a Jet Plane: A Perfect Storm of Recent Historical Events Would Make a Draft More Divisive and Dangerous Than Ever Before in the Nation's History," *Newsweek,* September 6, 2004.

Thomas E. Ricks, "Lukewarm on a Draft," *The Washington Post,* November 1, 2004.

Erik W. Robelen, "Draft Talk Worries A Generation That Hasn't Seen One," *Education Week,* November 3, 2004.

Donald H. Rumsfeld, remarks to Newspaper Association of American and American Society of Newspaper Editors, April 22, 2004.

Phyllis Schlafly, "Women Don't Belong in Ground Combat," Eagle Forum, June 1, 2005. www.eagleforum.org.

Doug Soderstrom, "A Reinstated Military Draft? Advice from an Old Man," *Common Dreams.org,* January 9, 2006.

Thomas Sowell, "A Military Draft?" *Townhall.com,* August 1, 2006.

John M. Swomley, "Draft May Reopen so War-Making Can Expand," *The Human Quest*, May-June 2004.

Aeon J. Skoble, "Neither Slavery Nor Involuntary Servitude," *Ideas on Liberty*, September 2003.

Cynthia Tucker, "Rich Pay Little for Freedom," *Atlanta Journal-Constitution*, May 30, 2004.

Kyle Tucker, "Back (Door) Stabbed," *Political Affairs*, April 2005.

Joan Vennochi, "A Military Draft Might Awaken Us," *Boston Globe*, June 22, 2006.

Walter Williams, "Reinstating the Military Draft," *Conservative Chronicle*, May 12, 2004.

Wilson Quarterly, "A Return to the Draft? A Survey of Recent Articles," Autumn 2005.

Evan M. Wooten, "Banging on the Backdoor Draft: The Constitutional Validity of Stop-Loss in the Military," *William and Mary Law Review*, December 1, 2005.

Web Sites

Draft Registration, Draft Resistance, the Military Draft, and the Medical Draft (http://hasbrouck.org/draft/). A comprehensive resource on military conscription and selective service in the United States. Provides historical background on the draft in the United States and answers questions to those wondering what might happen to them in the even of a draft.

FirstGov.gov—The U.S. Government's Official Web Portal (www.firstgov.gov). A one-stop site that provides information about federal government agencies and provides Internet links to agencies and programs.

National Archives Online Veteran and Military Documents (www.archives.gov/veterans/research/online.html). Provides a variety of veteran records and military documents including military documents, databases, online collections, and photographs.

Peace and Justice Support Network of Mennonite Church USA (peace.mennolink.org/youth). Produces information about recruitment and the draft including information for potential conscientious objectors and resource links.

Selective Service System (www.sss.gov). The Web site of the Selective Service System, an independent federal agency that oversees conscription of eligible individuals to serve in the military in the event of a need for extra manpower (such as a declaration of war). It is also charged with finding alternative service programs for anyone classified as a conscientious objector.

Stop the Draft.com (http://stopthedraft.com/index.php). A comprehensive anti-draft Web site with a plethora of articles culled from a variety of resources on why the draft should not be reinstated.

Index

Vanuatu, 91

Venezuela, 91

Veterans, 18–19

Veterans of Foreign Wars (VFW), 105

Vietnam War
  attitudes towards, 18, 24–26, 29, 31–32
  impact of, 7, 35, 39, 51–52, 63, 69, 76–78, 90

Violence, 11, 50–51, 55, 64

Volunteers, 7–10, 23, 25, 27, 33, 41–42, 78, 88

War, 9–10, 15, 22–23, 28–34, 36, 40, 51–52, 63–65

War on Terror, 7, 9–10, 13, 31, 64, 76

Weapons, 22, 27

Web sites, 59

Whites, 32, 37, 89

Winfrey, Oprah, 14

Wolfowitz, Paul, 51

World War I, 76, 90

World War II, 14, 16, 18, 22–26, 31, 33, 76, 90

Writing, 5, 58

Yemen, 91

Youth. *See also* Teenagers, 9, 14–17, 24, 34, 69–71

Zimbabwe, 91

Picture Credits

About the Editor

Lauri S. Friedman earned her bachelor's degree in religion and political science from Vassar College in Poughkeepsie, NY. Her studies there focused on political Islam. Friedman has worked as a non-fiction writer, a newspaper journalist, and an editor for more than 7 years. She has accumulated extensive experience in both academic and professional settings.

Friedman has edited and authored numerous publications for Greenhaven Press on controversial social issues such as gay marriage, Islam, energy, discrimination, suicide bombers, and the war on terror. Much of the *Writing the Critical Essay* series has been under her direction or authorship. She was instrumental in the creation of the series, and played a critical role in its conception and development.